PRAISE FOR
THE SEVEN DISCIPLINES
OF UNCOMMON
FREEDOM

"Every person has staggering potential, yet few realize it. Kevin Tinter, after guiding over 100,000 people toward improving their lives, has condensed those transformative principles into one remarkable volume. *The Seven Disciplines of Uncommon Freedom* is your roadmap to a life of significance, influence, and fulfillment beyond what many would dare to dream. I believe a single book can pivot your life—and this, my friends, could very well be that book."

John C. Maxwell
#1 New York Times Bestselling Author,
Coach, and Speaker

"An uncommon life begins the moment you take radical responsibility for it—which, sadly, is uncommon today. In *The Seven Disciplines of Uncommon Freedom*, Kevin Tinter will challenge you to live intentionally so you can rise above the norm and defy the status quo."

John Bevere

Best-selling Author, Minister, and
Co-founder of Messenger International and MessengerX

"You are welcome to read any self-help book by a Hollywood celebrity who has blossomed to fame and fortune through luck. But you will be so much more blessed to read *The Seven Disciplines of Uncommon Freedom* by Kevin Tinter. This is a story of a man from an average family who used his mind, faith, and God-given wisdom to not just bring himself success, but his friends and family as well. I am not inspired by athletes, celebrities, or trust fund babies. But I am greatly inspired by the guy next door who earned every penny through mindset, hard work, and a devotion to his path designed by God. I know you will be inspired, too. After all, Kevin didn't get wealthy and then live a life of ease and luxury. He led his community, his family, and his friends to abundance and knowledge. Then he wrote a book to encourage you to do the same. That, my friends, is an inspiration!"

Lindsey Graham

The Patriot Barbie | Keynote Speaker, Author,
Media Personality, and Entrepreneur

"*The Seven Disciplines of Uncommon Freedom* is a well-written and challenging book! With great stories and achievable steps, Kevin Tinter leads the reader through a whole life overhaul. From finances to family, from mindsets to microdosing adversity, this book will put anyone hungry for growth and transformation on a well-lit path to a better tomorrow. Kevin is not simply talking about how to do things better or more intentionally; he is showing you what he's done. He is leading like a lion and is sure to impart the courage needed to face yourself in the mirror. I wholeheartedly recommend this book to anyone who is ready to upgrade the important parts of their life."

Danny Silk

Author and President of Loving On Purpose

"*The Seven Disciplines of Uncommon Freedom* is your no-nonsense guide to intentional living. In a world where it's easier to succumb to society's standards, Kevin Tinter challenges us to press in for a life that's thriving in every area, from marriage to finances to spirituality. This is a must-read for anyone who's ready to step into greater freedom and leave a lasting impact."

Havilah Cunnington

Founder of Truth to Table

"Every non-fiction book worth reading should challenge you and cause you to think. *The Seven Disciplines of Uncommon Freedom* does just that! If you believe that life could be better or that you can do better then read this book. Whether you're stuck at the bottom or are already working toward an improved life, the pages of this book provide unparalleled steps, strategies, and solutions in key life areas to make your journey upstream possible. Through real-life examples and solid foundational concepts, you'll experience how a change in mindset will lead to a multiplying effect, creating immediate and long-term impact in your life. Not only will you benefit, but so will those you love!"

Miles Mettler

Author, PhD, and Ambassador for Focus on the Family

"Over the last decade, we've had a front row seat as we have coached and observed Kevin Tinter creating Uncommon Freedom for his family and the thousands of people he's coached. As you dive into the pages of this book, you will be empowered and equipped to create a life of purpose, significance, and abundance."

Doug and Thea Wood
Best-selling Authors, Coaches, and Entrepreneurs

"*The Seven Disciplines of Uncommon Freedom* is a remarkable guide that unveils the secret to living a truly fulfilling life, one that is marked by a harmonious blend of health, family, and prosperity. With profound wisdom and practical insights, Kevin Tinter takes readers on a transformative journey, teaching them how to intentionally architect their lives for ultimate success and happiness. From the very first page, this book captivates with its storytelling and relatable examples. The author's genuine passion for helping others shines through, making it easy to connect with the material on a personal level. *The Seven Disciplines of Uncommon Freedom* is a must-read for anyone seeking to live a purposeful, balanced, and prosperous life. Whether you are a young professional, a parent, or someone simply yearning for a more fulfilling life, *The Seven Disciplines of Uncommon Freedom* will guide you towards the extraordinary life you are designed to live."

Jared Roth Ed.D
President of Accelerate Business Coaching

"This book is a practical and tactical guide to defining, pursuing, and achieving meaningful success in every aspect of one's life. Kevin Tinter is vulnerable and courageous as he shares his hard-earned wisdom and a skillful framework for navigating the obstacles to optimizing our lives."

Richard Goerling
Founder of Mindful Badge Initiative,
Veteran, and Retired Police Lieutenant

UNCOMMON

THE SEVEN DISCIPLINES OF UNCOMMON FREEDOM

THE SEVEN DISCIPLINES OF UNCOMMON FREEDOM

Embrace Them to Reach Your Potential and Build a Life You Love

KEVIN TINTER

STORY ᶦᑊᶦᶦᑊᶦ CHORUS

THE SEVEN DISCIPLINES
OF UNCOMMON FREEDOM

Cover design by Pie in the Sky Studios
(www.pie-in-the-sky.com)

Published by
STORY ᯤ CHORUS
Learn more at www.StoryChorus.com

DEDICATION

This book is dedicated to the many people currently going "downstream" who will make the worthwhile decision to start swimming upstream after reading this book. When you join the small but mighty group rowing upstream, leading the great life we are all intended to live, you will become *uncommon*. The work of going against the current is hard but worth it, as uncommon freedom is only found upstream.

This book is also dedicated to the thousands of people who are the boots on the ground, serving Christ in amazing ministries and changing the world for the better: pregnancy care centers, family and parenting ministries, water well drilling ministries, and legal ministries defending those being persecuted for their faith and those trying to preserve the God-given freedoms our founding fathers intended us to have. I've heard it said that all it takes for evil to triumph is for good people to do nothing. My prayer for this book is that it inspires good people to work toward uncommon freedom, thereby prompting a wave of wealth creation and generous donations of at least 100 million dollars in new giving, equipping you to continue the hard work you are already doing.

TABLE OF CONTENTS

FOREWORD

Are you ready for your next? This is an open-ended question I believe you will find the answer to as you read this book! I once heard it said that time stands still for no man. Now more than ever, I understand this statement. We must embrace our God-assigned purpose and do our best to leave a legacy worthy of hearing the words, "well done."

Oftentimes, the hand we are dealt can destroy potential and purpose before personal maturity awakens the soul. That is why I believe we all need this book. My friend, author Kevin Tinter, has written this powerful book as a compass for your life's journey. *Uncommon Freedom* is a game changer not only for the focused leader but also for the rudderless sojourner seeking direction.

First, let me share some insight on the author. I am honored to call Kevin Tinter my friend. Not only is he a man of integrity and compassion, but he is also one of the most profound problem-solving thinkers of our generation. I have had the joy of being in many corporate meetings where Kevin has helped strategically and confidently guide the entire room toward resolution. Kevin is a man with a deep faith who lives his life boldly. He and his wife, Bekah, believe that they are on this earth to restore hope to the hopeless. They know that God has anointed them for such a time as this! My friend is a patriot who stands on the wall awaiting his next assignment. I share all of that to simply say: When Kevin talks,

I listen. I lean in and always leave a better man. As the wisdom of Proverbs 3:13 (NKJV) states, "Happy is the man who finds wisdom, and the man who gains understanding."

I want to warn you in advance to prepare your spirit for a heart and mind shift as you read this book. I have learned that conviction comes when the heart is open to change. As I read this book, I was moved on several occasions to evaluate my personal life and make course corrections. This book will call you to be accountable for the dash on your tombstone. There will be moments when you must look under the microscope to study your personal life anatomy of self-governance or pick up a telescope to see where you must go next to achieve the purpose that God planned for you. The great thing is that Kevin gives us a simple formula for success.

This is a legacy book that is needed at this exact moment in time. Now more than ever in our history, we must find those with conviction for absolute truth who will decide to be louder than the noisy culture and choose to walk in boldness to confront the obstacles that have held them back. This is your invitation to "do a redesign" and experience the power of "Uncommon Freedom!"

Pat Schatzline
Author, Evangelist, and CEO
of 2CD LLC and Remnant Ministries International

A NOTE FROM BEKAH

Dear Kev,

You did it! I never doubted that you could, but I did wonder how long it might take . . . just kidding. You have more integrity than any other person I know. When you make a commitment, you are compelled to follow through.

The last twenty-five-plus years have been full of laughter, growth, contending, heartbreak, purpose, community, and massive wins. I'm so grateful we've been able to walk all of this together. I'm more in love with you each year, and I respect the way you continue to grow in every area of life.

Your love for Jesus is your internal compass, your passion for freedom creates an unquenchable desire for more impact, and your love for others is the fuel that keeps you going.

I'm so proud of the work you put into documenting, learning, and sharing these incredible principles that continue to serve our lives in parenting, marriage, faith, finances, and business. Stewardship is one of our guiding principles and you have been so faithful, my love.

I cannot wait to see what God does with this message, and I will forever be your biggest fan.

Love,
Bek

CHAPTER 1

THE SEVEN DISCIPLINES OF UNCOMMON FREEDOM

There's not much in my background that signaled I'd have the lifestyle I do today. Growing up, we were the one-car family on a block where everyone had two, and our rusty, green 1972 Gran Torino wasn't much. I remember a time when I was squished between my brothers on our way to church in the back seat of our battered car. My mom pulled up in front of a neighbor's house to pick up my father for church. As he ducked into the packed-full car, I tapped on his knee, warning him to watch out for the rusted-out hole in the floor. It was my job to keep the floor mat covering the rusted hole, so it was also my job to warn anyone new that it existed.

My father was a music teacher in the public school system, and when that didn't make ends meet, he moonlighted as a wedding and sports photographer. This often meant that his Saturdays were spent away from the family. I can still see my mother sitting at the dinner table in the evening light, cobbling the finances together. I remember thinking, even as a little kid, I didn't want this to be my future. Still, our parents worked hard, kept a roof over our heads, and made sure our bellies were full—no small task when you're raising four boys.

My days were mostly happy, filled with wrestling my three brothers, playing catch in the yard, watching the Cleveland Browns (usually lose), and, of course, any moment of TV we could talk our parents into letting us watch. For me, the gold standard of entertainment was *CHiPs*. I loved watching "Ponch" and Baker scream across the California highways on their motorcycles to catch the bad guys. They were real-life heroes, and somewhere a seed was planted. I wanted to be a cop just like them when I grew up.

Try finding a photo of me as a child without wearing my toy six-shooter at my hip. It's nearly impossible because that toy gun went with me everywhere. When we went to pick my grandparents up at the airport, I had to leave it at the security desk, which was a little traumatizing for a kid. Whether it was the toy gun or a stick I picked up, I was ready to defend. The other toy I almost carried as much as the six shooter was a hammer, and so from an early age, my personality was about building and defending.

Twenty years later, I was suiting up for my first patrol on the Hillsboro Police Department in Hillsboro, Oregon.

Defending, protecting and building were in my blood from my youth.

Working with my dad on their house remodel circa 1998.

While my patrols weren't filled with the high-speed chases and silver screen drama I'd grown up watching, I loved being a cop. I never would've guessed it, but my favorite work ended up being enforcing DUIs.

My Aunt Kim joined me for a ride-along circa 2011.

It doesn't take long to see the telltale signs of someone driving under the influence of alcohol or drugs. Every night on DUI patrol I went through some version of these ten steps:

STEP ONE:
Pull over a swerving vehicle.

STEP TWO:
Approach the vehicle.

STEP THREE:
Look a bleary-eyed driver in the eyes as they crammed two sticks of Big Red in their mouth to kill the smell of alcohol.

STEP FOUR:
Ask: "Driver's license and registration, please."

STEP FIVE:
Watch their shaky, uncoordinated hands struggle to produce the documents.

STEP SIX:
Ask: "How many drinks have you had tonight?"

STEP SEVEN:
Listen to their response: "Only a couple of drinks at dinner, oc-ifer . . . ."

STEP EIGHT:
Ask: "Would you step out of the car for me, please?"

STEP NINE:
Watch them mysteriously lose all balance and forget how to walk in a straight line.

STEP TEN:
Arrest, book, repeat.

It wasn't glamorous work—and it certainly wasn't cool enough to get its own *episode* of CHiPs—but it made a genuine difference. We were told that we saved one life for every ten drunk drivers pulled off the road. So this work directly saved thousands *of* lives and gave me that satisfying sense of justice being served. Every arrest was one less individual putting the lives of innocent people at risk just because they couldn't call a cab.

Not everything about police work was this satisfying, but it was still a great fit for a working-class Ohio kid like me. However, things changed as my wife, Bekah, and I began having kids. Shift by shift, the job consumed progressively more of my life. After all, as our family grew, so did our expenses. So I started taking overtime shifts every chance I got to make ends meet.

On many weekends I would leave the house quietly before sunrise on Friday morning and work almost 48 hours straight. Then, I'd return home to catch a few hours' sleep before another shift began. I was constantly exhausted from picking up extra shifts—and to this day, I hate driving tired because of how many times I slapped myself in the face to stay awake in my patrol car.

Holidays melted from happy celebrations to stressful occasions faster than Handel's ice cream on a hot summer sidewalk. Christmas mornings were depressing. I had just enough time to open a few presents with my wife and kids before I had to be back on patrol. The Fourth of July was more of the same. My family went to the parade without me and then to the backyard barbeque where I would show up late. And even when I was home, all I could think about was the clock counting down until my early-morning alarm would scream at me to get back to work.

The thing was, I didn't just log the overtime for the money. Bekah was pregnant with our third child, Dylan. And because our department was stretched thin, getting time off was nearly impossible—even eight or nine months was insufficient lead time for so much as a family wedding. So if I wanted any quality time with my family once the baby came, I had to strategically bank hours to combine with the family leave I was guaranteed.

During this stretch my physical health took a nosedive, deteriorating beneath the mountains of extra hours in a cop car.

NOT EVERYTHING
ABOUT POLICE WORK
WAS THIS SATISFYING,
BUT IT WAS STILL
A GREAT FIT FOR A
WORKING-CLASS OHIO
KID LIKE ME.

As a police officer, the deck is already stacked against your health when you spend most of your time driving around and eating like crap (donuts are a police stereotype for a reason). And then of course officers have to lash the top-heavy utility belt and chest protection onto themselves, so our backs don't stand a chance. It wasn't a huge surprise when an officer needed back surgery.

Unfortunately, I was one of those officers, having my first back surgery at thirty years old. The extra work I was putting in left little time for exercise, healthy eating, or even sleep. Plus, I now carried around an extra thirty pounds of Krispy Kremes and french fries. At that point, I accepted that a second back surgery awaited me in the not-too-distant future, and there wasn't anything I could do about it.

You'd think that with all this extra work I was putting in, things would get easier on the financial side. But that never seemed to happen. The truth was, I was overworked, overweight, and overwhelmed. I couldn't make headway. Balance was a laughable concept. And I was trapped in a never-ending cycle of working myself to the bone, only to be rewarded with more penny-pinching while I missed out on time with my family.

My childhood dream had become a waking nightmare. I was trading the most important years of my life for twenty-five dollars an hour and the promise of a pension nearly thirty years in the future. The idea of freedom, of options, of any autonomy at all, seemed sequestered behind the iron gates of retirement. I didn't think I could make it that long. Things needed to change, but I didn't know how.

THIS IS WHERE THINGS CHANGE

The Kevin you just met, the cop hustling to bank PTO, the guy trading hours for dollars, the dad kicking himself for missing his kids' lives, the husband who wished he could invest more energy into his marriage . . . . That was a man who knew what he wanted and was willing to do whatever it took to get it.

But my problem wasn't inspiration, it was navigation. I had the necessary drive, determination, and grit, but I couldn't crack the secret code for getting ahead.

If you can relate at all, I'm glad you picked up this book. Because I discovered that the dream of owning my time instead of slogging through extra shifts was actually possible. The financial abundance to give generously to the causes my wife and I are passionate about could happen. The opportunity to thrive instead of just survive wasn't beyond my reach. And rather than putting my freedom on layaway, we could build a life we didn't need to retire from. Today, Bekah and I call this a life of uncommon freedom—and it's our central mission to help anyone who wants to achieve it.

Uncommon freedom is the ability to do what you want, when you want, with whom you want, while making the world a better place. Put simply, it's a pipe *dream* that can come true. There are no magic wands to wave. No get-rich-quick schemes to buy into. No cheat codes to shortcut the process. But there are principles that always work—as long as you do.

If you truly want change, this is where it can happen. It's where it happened for us.

It blows my mind to share this, but last year our charitable giving alone equaled what I would have made working full-time plus overtime during my entire career as a cop. I don't share this to brag or pat myself on the back. Instead, I share it to encourage you. Because if an average guy like me can find the path to uncommon freedom, I believe you can, too.

While it took Bekah and me years of trial and error and being blessed with some incredible relationships and opportunities to figure it out, you don't have to do that. I'm going to share everything I would love to have known then. I'm writing the book

I wish someone would've handed me so many years ago in my cop car.

And the first lesson? A powerful concept I learned during my tenure as a Marine Corps officer prior to becoming a police officer: commander's intent.

COMMANDER'S INTENT

The commander's intent outlines your senior leader's desired end state. It's a simple statement that helps everyone down the chain of command understand what they're there to accomplish. This way, when plans have to change, the troops on the ground can improvise while still making progress toward the ultimate goal. It's the unchanging North Star guiding forward progress when the crap hits the fan—and it always does.

In 2004, while serving on deployment in Okinawa, Japan, my commanding officer (C.O.) called me into his office. They were calling for a handful of Marines to support the Iraq War effort stateside, and it turned out I was one of them.

Graduating from Marine Corps Officer Candidate School in Quantico, VA in August, 2000.

"You're leaving in a month," he said. And that was that.

Bekah and I had been married for a few years at this point, and we were just settling into life in Okinawa. We loved it there. We had an awesome church, a great community, and plenty of purpose. But I was a Marine, and it was time to fulfill my wartime duty. While I always imagined I'd be deployed to fight in Iraq, the Marine Corps had other plans.

When I arrived at Camp Pendleton in California, I learned I would work as a First Lieutenant for General James Mattis—one of the most respected (and feared) commanders in modern military history. General Mattis has led Marines in every major conflict since 1990, from the Persian Gulf War to the wars in the Middle East. He oversaw the longest sustained overland advance in Marine Corps history during the Iraq War and even sat at the right hand of former President Donald Trump as Secretary of Defense. He's a man among men—and certainly not someone to disappoint.

At the beginning of my assignment, he made it clear there was no margin for error. Mattis was known for firing full-bird colonels in the field in an instant for poor performance.

I was the casualty tracking officer for the 1st Marine Division, which meant I was responsible for tracking and reporting every single one of our casualties in Iraq. That division included over 6,500 Marines. My job was to have real-time, perfectly accurate information available twenty-four hours a day, seven days a week for General Mattis.

It didn't matter if someone died in the line of duty or got a papercut filling out reports. If it happened in the theater of war, we documented it. The real trick wasn't documenting an incident—it was tracking the Marine. General Mattis didn't simply want to know what happened to Private So-and-So, he wanted to know what flight brought him home, what hospital he was in, and what his prognosis was. And this was all after our team personally called his family.

On my initial day on the job as a First Lieutenant, a captain was my direct report, so I checked in with her right away. She said the job would be a cakewalk. This war was going to be a lopsided victory with only a sprained ankle or two. My staff non-commissioned officer (SNCO) was Gunnery Sergeant Mike Roth, a seasoned Marine who knew the captain was going to be wrong on this. Always listen to your gunny!

The situation in the city of Fallujah proved her wrong and Gunnery Sergeant Roth right.

Operation Valiant Resolve, the military code name for the battles in Fallujah, lasted over a month with the insurgents fighting fiercely, resulting in a drawn-out and bloody conflict no one expected. My unit was swamped with personnel casualty reports to process. As the casualties mounted, I quickly realized that we needed to radically shift the process. If we didn't, we wouldn't have the moment-by-moment information that General Mattis required.

We weren't about to disappoint him.

Luckily, fate provided me with one of the best leaders I've ever worked with, Lieutenant Colonel Rob Kosid. He basically said, "Kevin, here's the mission. Get the job done." He took a hands-off approach and let me do the work exactly how I felt it needed to be done.

The problem we faced was we needed to work day and night to match the casualty numbers pouring in. Standard procedure wasn't going to cut it. But because we knew our commander's intent, we improvised, working outside the box to create a fireman-type schedule. We split the shifts up so someone was awake and entering data every hour of the day. Necessity preceded innovation, and our 24/7 Casualty Operations Center became the standard for all the Casualty Operations in the Marine Corps. We recorded, tracked, and reported over 2,400 casualties, and were responsible for facilitating the proper notification of the sometimes heartbreaking news to their families, either by phone or in person, depending on the level of injury.

When you understand your commander's intent, it doesn't matter how much reality deviates from your plan. All that matters is you adapt and keep working to fulfill your mission. But you don't have to be a Marine to apply the commander's intent. Because there's a higher echelon of leaders we all report to, far beyond even a four-star general: the creator of the universe Himself.

PROSPERITY WITH A PURPOSE

I grew up in a Christian home. We went to church on Sundays and youth group on Wednesdays, and I read my Bible and prayed— though not as consistently as I should have. And even though I never had a "wandering" season where I questioned my faith, I did always wrestle with the question: What is God's purpose for me?

For some, they get their answer in a singular moment of clarity. For me, it came more slowly, layer by layer. My drive to be a police officer, to serve in the military, to care for my family, and now today, helping hundreds of thousands of people get healthier and build a better life, are all signposts. I believe God made me to protect, provide, and prosper:

1. Protect the vulnerable.

2. Provide for my family and help others do the same for theirs.

3. Prosper not for my benefit alone but to do the greatest good I'm capable of doing in the world.

Purpose is unique to each of us. God gives us all different gifts, callings, and starting points. However, we do each share a fundamental directive—God's original commander's intent. That purpose shares the common denominator of Genesis 1:28: "Then

God blessed them and said, 'Be fruitful and multiply. Fill the earth and govern it. Reign over the fish in the sea, the birds in the sky, and all the animals that scurry along the ground.'"

From the beginning, God gave humanity a multiplication mandate. We weren't called to sit in the garden sipping fruity drinks with umbrellas. We were called to bring order to chaos so creation could flourish. From fish to ferns, God made us stewards.

Stewardship means we don't own what we have; we're caretakers. In a literal sense, everything you and I have has been entrusted to us by the true Owner. And as we'll continue digging into, the Owner isn't interested in things staying the same as the way we got them. He expects us to multiply our impact with all we've been given—from our possessions to our innate abilities to the opportunities in our path. Fundamentally, multiplication is God's Commander's Intent. The Great Commission calls us to make more disciples. The Parable of the Talents calls us to multiply our time, talent, and treasure. And in the parlance of uncommon freedom, we call this "prosperity with a purpose."

Our prosperity with a purpose: creating Arizona's first mobile pregnancy resource center.

It is our responsibility to achieve the greatest abundance (prosperity) in every area of life to create the greatest impact (purpose) for God's kingdom. To be transparent, my goal with this book is to inspire ridiculous generosity. I want this book to inspire

100 million dollars of new giving to causes aligned with the Gospel. Honestly, that type of giving only takes one hundred millionaires to give 10 percent for ten years. We can probably accomplish this goal together in less than five. Are you ready to become the next purpose-driven millionaire?

Proverbs 29:2 (NIV) puts it best: "When the righteous thrive, the people rejoice; when the wicked rule, the people groan." Uncommon freedom is a path to fulfilling that promise, helping God's people thrive to advance the kingdom.

If you're in for the journey, that's what we will spend the rest of this book pursuing together.

THE SEVEN DISCIPLINES OF UNCOMMON FREEDOM

Uncommon freedom means thriving in seven distinct areas: health, wealth, marriage, family, community, spirituality, and lifestyle.

As I said, it is the freedom to do what you want, when you want, with whom you want, all with kingdom purpose.

We must reach our full potential to achieve it. And when we do, we maximize our impact.

Seven disciplines guide the pursuit of uncommon freedom and they always work when applied consistently and correctly. They are the physics of achievement. In the rest of this book, we will dig deeper into each. To start, let's do a flyover of where we're headed.

DISCIPLINE ONE: GET YOUR BODY ON MISSION

Your health is the first hill to take. Without it, we have a weakened capacity for impact. I've watched too many people sacrifice their health to get wealth . . . only to use that money to regain their health at the end of their lives. An object at rest tends to stay at rest, and an object in motion tends to stay in motion. We're going to get our bodies into motion. Maximizing your physical health will give you the energy to perform at your best in every facet of life.

Discipline one is getting your body on mission.

DISCIPLINE TWO: MASTER YOURSELF, MASTER YOUR WEALTH

Everything we need to know about wealth can be distilled to one word: stewardship. The Bible is filled with masterful lessons on the concept. From multiplying what we've been given, to harnessing the compound effect, to living below our means, to God's blessing upon our generosity—stewardship means resisting debt, impulse, and lack of discipline. Francis Bacon put it best: "Money is a great servant but a bad master."

Uncommon freedom actively loves God by making money through stewardship and using money for stewardship. In this context, poverty is no virtue and wealth is no vice.

Therefore, discipline two is mastering ourselves in order to master our wealth.

DISCIPLINE THREE: BUILD A BULLETPROOF MARRIAGE

The average marriage lasts only eight years.[1] The third discipline is squarely aimed at making sure this doesn't become your story because a bulletproof marriage is essential to uncommon

---

1. "Divorce Rate in the United States Since 1990," Statista, accessed February 12, 2023, https://www.statista.com/statistics/195955/divorce-rate-in-the-united-states-since-1990/.

YOU NEED PEOPLE IN
YOUR LIFE WHO WILL
PUSH AND SUPPORT
YOU IN THE HUNT FOR
UNCOMMON FREEDOM.

freedom. After all, one of the first things we're told God said was it's not good for humans to be alone (Genesis 2:18). Marriage is fundamental to raising godly future generations and is even a facet of how we relate to God—with husbands loving our wives as Christ loves the Church (Ephesians 5:25). No marriage will be perfect, because people aren't perfect. But this most important relationship can always be better.

Discipline three is building a bulletproof marriage.

DISCIPLINE FOUR: PARENT WITH A PURPOSE

C.S. Lewis was spot on when he said, "Children are not a distraction from work, they are the most important work." No positive impact you make can balance out the weight you put on society if you neglect your children. Our children will form their first impressions of how they see God through our interactions with them, so it is our sacred duty to raise them well. Our purpose as parents isn't simply to make our kids happy or raise well-adjusted children. Instead, we're raising them to be godly adults, productive citizens, and better spouses and parents than we are today.

Discipline four is learning how to parent with purpose.

DISCIPLINE FIVE: RUN WITH LIONS

I can't overstate the importance of finding community with people who inspire, challenge, and mentor you. I have always believed that you find greatness in pockets of community. Show me your friends and I'll show you your future. You need people in your life who will push and support you in the hunt for uncommon freedom. That's why we run with lions instead of hanging with donkeys. This discipline will make you or break you—because it works in both directions.

Discipline five is running with lions.

DISCIPLINE SIX: HONOR THE KING

Nothing empties heaven's storeroom of blessing like honoring God first in all things. He blesses what we dedicate to His purposes. And I can promise you this: You cannot out-give, out-serve, or out-love God. Proverbs 9:10 (NIV) shares the secret: "The fear of the LORD is the beginning of wisdom, and knowledge of the Holy One is understanding." Fear doesn't mean running in terror. It means awe, reverence, respect, and honor for One Who is far greater than ourselves. This is why we honor God with our bank accounts, relationships, children, bodies, and everything else He's given us.

Discipline six is honoring God first in everything we do and all that we are.

DISCIPLINE SEVEN: DESIGN YOUR LIFE

Uncommon freedom is for people who are determined to build the life they want rather than accept the live they were given. I personally know the difference between surviving and thriving, and designing the life you want begins long before we are "thriving" on paper. Lifestyle design is not for the materially wealthy, it's for the people who want to be the dominant force in their own lives. The disciplines of uncommon freedom work together to give us both the ability and the guardrails to do this well.

Discipline seven is designing the life we don't need a vacation from.

BECOME UNCOMMON

Now that you know where we're headed, here are the brass tacks on where many of us are today:

About 70 percent of Americans are overweight or obese—unhealthy is normal. Be uncommon.

The average American carries a $6,194 credit card balance—debt is normal. Be uncommon.

Over 50 percent of marriages end in divorce—separation is normal. Be uncommon.

Half of our children grow up without dads in their homes—fatherlessness is normal. Be uncommon.

Many have friends and colleagues that drag them down—relational poverty is normal. Be uncommon.

Less than 20 percent of American Christians actually read their Bible—spiritual starvation is normal. Be uncommon.

Most accept the life they're given rather than build the life of their dreams—accepting the status quo is normal. Be uncommon.

When guided by the seven disciplines, uncommon clarity, drive, and habits build a life of uncommon freedom.

But I've stumbled. I didn't figure out everything perfectly right from the start.

However, I have learned some powerful lessons along the way—one of the most important being the people who finish upstream are the ones who never quit rowing.

So let's make a deal: I'll share everything I know, and you show up with everything you've got. If a blue-collar kid from Ohio can make it this far, so can you. The seven disciplines don't fail. However, there's something beneath the surface that makes them work. Without them, our effort is doomed to failure.

Let's dive into what holds it all together: the trinity of uncommon freedom.

CHAPTER 2

THE TRINITY OF
UNCOMMON FREEDOM

There are no shortcuts. Just ask the Donner party.

Lansford Hastings was a former Confederate soldier turned explorer, and he promoted the Hastings Cutoff. He claimed it was a shortcut across Utah (and some treacherous terrain) to get to California. To encourage people to come, Hastings wrote a guidebook giving directions to settlers called *The Emigrants' Guide to Oregon and California.*

Unfortunately, Hastings hadn't fully traveled the described route himself, nor had he done it in difficult weather. People believed him, based on his name and reputation, and the Donner party was persuaded to take his shortcut.

We all know how that turned out.

You cannot find an easy way to get to the things that matter the most; there is no shortcut to them, no way to avoid the hard work. Transforming your life into one of uncommon freedom takes work.

The good news?

There are only three things you must remember. They're not shortcuts, but they are direct routes.

THE POWER OF THREE

The Parthenon has stood on the Acropolis, towering over Athens, for nearly 2,500 years.

Its Doric columns and carefully balanced facade illustrate near-perfection in high classical Greek art and architecture. Earthquakes, wars, storms, scavengers, and relic hunters have come and gone, and yet it still stands.

How did ancient Greek engineers build a structure so enduring when other buildings of antiquity and even of today haven't fared as well? They didn't have the benefit of strong Roman concrete yet. How did they manage to build something so strong with limited technology?

As it turns out, three secrets hold the key to this iconic structure's longevity.

Engineers call it "triple insulation," and as the name implies, it's a combination of three ingenious techniques.[2]

SECRET ONE: FIRM FOUNDATION.
They built the Parthenon on natural, layered marble slabs, forming a foundation capable of absorbing the earth's seismic activity.

SECRET TWO: POWERFUL CONNECTIONS.
The architects used lead joints that absorb the powerful, damaging vibrations from earthquakes that typically topple structures.

SECRET THREE: PERFECT-FIT PILLARS.
Rather than solid columns, the pillars are actually cut into perfectly fitting slices, allowing them to flex with the rest of the structure.

This is the power of three.

You don't need *a lot* to get *a lot*. You just need three of the right things, in the right combinations, to get more out of the final result.

Like the Parthenon's triple insulation, or the Father, Son, and Holy Spirit, or the unbreakable strand of three cords described in Ecclesiastes 4:12, we're going to unpack the three components that are sturdy enough to support a remarkable life. I call them

---

2. Philip Chrysopoulos, "How the Parthenon was Built to Withstand Anything," Greek Reporter, May 13, 2023, https://greekreporter.com/2023/05/13/pathenon-construction-engineering/.

YOU DON'T NEED *A LOT* TO GET *A LOT*. YOU JUST NEED THREE OF THE RIGHT THINGS, IN THE RIGHT COMBINATIONS, TO GET MORE OUT OF THE FINAL RESULT.

the trinity of uncommon freedom, and without them in place, the seven disciplines won't last.

The trinity is comprised of these three directives:

1. Always row upstream
2. Get to one
3. Upgrade your circle

If the seven disciplines act as the pillars supporting a life of uncommon freedom, these three directives are the foundation. If any of them are missing, cracking, or eroding, everything tumbles eventually.

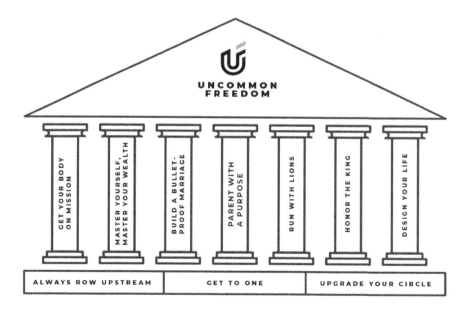

A life of uncommon freedom is only achieved by understanding and applying this trinity. So let's examine each and learn to harness this incredible power.

ALWAYS ROW UPSTREAM

There's a reason they call it a lazy river.

Hop on the inner tube and float around wherever the current takes you. No need to be bothered with oars or anything that would help you steer. There's no real requirement for you; you don't even have to keep your head above the water, because the tube will do that for you. Just close your eyes, bask in the sun, and end up somewhere. Let the moving water around you make the decision on where that might be.

We're surrounded by lazy rivers. It seems everyone has one to offer, whether you choose it or fall into it by accident. Our environment is not naturally pulling us toward freedom, though it might convince you for a long time that you're still having a pretty good ride.

Until the rapids.

Until the waterfall.

Until the sandbar.

You can easily end up in divorce, financial ruin, and isolation from your community if you let the current decide where you'll go. The journey to uncommon freedom doesn't use an inner tube to reach inner peace. In fact, that journey won't even start until you get in the boat and start rowing.

In life, we tend to float downstream and end up where everyone else ends up, along with whatever garbage was in that river. Downstream is the convenient way, the way of least resistance, the way of those who are too tired or distracted or busy to do anything else. Downstream is the way of the procrastinator who will make important changes tomorrow.

Take health, for example.

We live in an obesogenic society where everything in our surrounding environment encourages us to be obese.

Cheap calories are everywhere. Food and drinks are used as rewards, enticement, and as a distraction. Cheap calories are offered to fix every problem. Bored? Anxious? Sad? Hungry? The current carries you right toward the things that will destroy your health.

Rowing upstream when it comes to your health means purposefully choosing less or no alcohol and healthier food. It means choosing to get off your butt, and taking the stairs instead of the elevator. The key word is *choosing*. A life without purposeful decisions is a life on the lazy river, because no decision is still a decision.

When it comes to finances, easy credit and buy now, pay later schemes are the downstream currents pulling you right over the waterfall and into financial ruin. If you've been there, you know the sound of the roaring waterfall (maybe it's blood rushing to your brain in a panic) when the bills arrive. You can see the rapids ahead as you juggle them, paying some and not others, changing your phone number once again to ward off collection agents. Debt has complete control of you, and your entire existence feels like you're in service to that debt. Rowing upstream with your finances means you stop spending more money than you have and make saving, instead of spending, your habit.

With relationships, a trip down the lazy river is easy to slip into. It's letting a screen be the babysitter and boss of your kids, instead of you. It's neglecting your spouse, never taking a date night because you're too tired or busy. It's letting relationships cool and coast without putting hard work into maintaining (and sometimes repairing) them. It's thinking that people are there to serve you and make your life better, allowing bitterness and anger to set in when you feel that others aren't doing enough for you. It's becoming a victim prone to complaining instead of a vital friend prone to encouraging.

Rowing upstream means choosing to spend intentional, quality time with the people you love. It means thinking of ways to serve and bless others. It doesn't insist that people fill in all the gaps in your life that only God can fill.

And speaking of God, drifting downstream in your spiritual life is probably the most agonizing experience in life because there's a kind of vague, unsettled feeling that starts in your gut, growing outward before you realize what the source of the problem is. When you're spiritually adrift, every turn in the lazy river brings anxiety and envy. Spiritual drifting can seem like a lot of other things, and so we throw a lot at it: pleasure, money, distraction, new purchases, new experiences. Spiritual drifting tugs on all the rest.

Rowing upstream spiritually means choosing to spend time in God's word every day, and spending time in constant prayer and God-conversation throughout the day.

UPSTREAM SOLUTIONS

When people ask me for advice, I am surprised at how many are looking for downstream solutions to their upstream problems.

Maybe your job isn't paying enough to support your family. That's a downstream problem. And you make it worse when you continue cruising downstream and think the solution is somewhere around the next bend, somewhere along the way the current is taking you. So you spend time paddling in circles, working extra hours, and begging for a raise when the better solution might be to row upstream to a new opportunity.

Remember, everyone and everything in that river is headed in the same direction. Some good, sure, but also the bad. So many issues that fester in our lives can't be solved in any way other than taking an oar and heading in a different direction.

Not convinced?

Imagine you're in a boat and you suddenly realize there's a baby in the water, floating by you. One moment you were enjoying a boat ride, the next you were horrified. Quickly rushing over, paddling as furiously as you can, you reach down and pull the baby out of the water. Problem solved.

But a few minutes later, your relief turns to horror when you see *another* infant bobbing along in the waves. You start over to save her, and just as you reach down to pull her to safety in the boat, you spot another baby in the water. Before long, you have a boat full of screaming, crying babies, your arms ache, you're completely soaked, and you feel little beyond exhaustion. It's then that you make out a figure standing along the shoreline.

Relieved, you paddle over to where they're standing and explain—over the racket of all the screaming babies—what's been going on. You ask for help rescuing them.

The stranger has other ideas, changing the entire situation with one simple question.

"Why don't we go upstream and find out why the babies are falling into the water?"

You have to go upstream and tackle the heart of the problem. Upstream problems are never solved downstream.

But I see people trying to solve things downstream all the time. Their efforts are heroic to watch—exhausting, even—but I know it's futile and it's hard to see them struggle. Rowing in circles, pulling screaming babies out of the water, working past exhaustion to pick up extra shifts and second and third jobs, getting nowhere, and sliding further downstream when they try to catch their breath. They're locked in permanent crisis mode.

All the downstream hustle in the world will never solve an upstream problem.

GRIT WITH A COMPASS

Grit is not enough.

You need grit, but finding uncommon freedom isn't a journey with a single route. Grit alone won't get you there. As a cop, I saw lots of people with grit rowing really hard in the *wrong* direction.

ALL THE
DOWNSTREAM
HUSTLE IN THE
WORLD WILL
NEVER SOLVE
AN UPSTREAM
PROBLEM.

Rest assured that criminals aren't necessarily lazy people; many have just as strong a desire to achieve as the next person. Waking up in the middle of the night, breaking into a house, sneaking about in the dark, and stealing valuables takes grit.

However, grit applied in the wrong direction will send you hurtling downstream.

Proverbs 10:4 (NIV) tells us "Lazy hands make for poverty, but diligent hands bring wealth." The obvious meaning here is that you have to work hard to accomplish anything of value. But when you dig into the original Hebrew, you find that the root of the word *diligent* is actually "to pick or choose out."

It doesn't just mean to work hard.

It means you have to make conscious decisions. You must choose the *right* work to put your energy into.

I could put in as many overtime hours as I wanted as a police officer, but that was me rowing in circles. Or, I could take a step back and get a sense of where I was heading compared to where I should go.

Getting anywhere worthwhile takes grit. But when you want to know how to get to that Promised Land, you also need a compass.

The reason so many people haven't found uncommon freedom isn't because they're lazy. It isn't because they lack grit. It's because they're going in the wrong direction. They might have a paddle and they're frantically rowing, but they don't see all the options that are open to them.

The right direction is against the current. The right direction for the problem is upstream. But once you start, you can't stop rowing. The water is working against you; if you stop, you drift downstream again.

Many people paddle hard at first, gathering a little momentum and hoping it's enough to let them coast the rest of the way, forgetting the current is always moving and that's why stopping doesn't work. No champion ever said, "Wow! That workout was so effective, I'll never have to do it again!" If you rest on the laurels of past success, all you're doing is losing what you gained.

Find the right direction and keep rowing, because you can't stop if you want uncommon freedom. I'm not going to sugarcoat this, but . . . .

You can't be healthy at any weight.

You can't be wealthy with a negative net worth.

You can't have a great marriage if you're disconnected.

You can't be the parent you want to be if you never spend time with your kids.

This is the hard truth.

I'm not saying you should be a workaholic and ignore what God has commanded us about rest. You absolutely can rest in God, but you absolutely can't rest in the lazy river. You absolutely can't rest in the exhausting, dirty current full of all the problems that will lead you to destruction.

There are seasons in life where rowing hard simply looks different.

Sometimes it feels like you're not making any progress, and you're working with all your strength simply to avoid losing ground. Maybe a medical catastrophe strikes or a loved one is lost.

It's during stormy weather that rowing hard might look different than it does when it's sunny. This is why you need people in the boat with you to keep you from going downstream when you need to take a break. For when you need to pull your oars out of the water for a time. Whether you're rowing and gaining ground, or you're pausing to grieve and catch your breath, the people you surround yourself with and place in your circle can keep you from losing ground.

Moses led God's people through the waters and the wilderness to the edge of the Promised Land. Paul tells us to keep our eye on the prize and press forward. George Washington literally rowed upstream through frozen water to strike a key victory for America's independence.

Significant impacts are always upstream, against the current. Row in the right direction. Because when you give it your all, you start to shift from placing a negative value on your life to giving it a positive value. This concept is called Get to One.

GET TO ONE

The Master in Matthew 25:14-30 had three servants, and just before he left on a long trip, he had them come to him. Lining them up, he started handing out massive amounts of cash (called talents). The first one received five bags. The second one received two bags. The third one received one bag.

"I'm giving you these talents based on your abilities," he told them. "I'm trusting you with my wealth." And then he left them there, holding their bags of gold.

The first servant turned five bags into ten. The second servant turned two bags into four. The third servant, out of fear, had buried his bag of gold with nothing but worry driving him. He wasn't about to gamble and lose anything; a safer path was best.

When the Master returned, he called his servants in and asked them to give an account of what they had done with his wealth. He was very pleased with the first two servants and rewarded them.

"Well done! You have been faithful with a few things, so I am going to put you in charge of many things," he told them. "Come and share in my happiness!"

The third servant, however, was another story.

When asked what he'd done with the gold entrusted to him, the servant dropped his head a bit as the fear rushed in. What had seemed like a good idea earlier—the easier, safer path—suddenly seemed like a bad idea.

"I was afraid of you," he admitted. "I hid your gold in the ground."

The Master was furious. "You wicked and lazy servant!" he said before sending him off for punishment. "Give his gold to the one who has ten bags of gold. For whoever has will be given more, and they will have an abundance. Whoever does not have, even what they have will be taken from them."

Wow.

That seems harsh, doesn't it? What should we make of this story?

In Matthew 25:14–30, where this parable that Jesus told is found, we learn how the foundational concept of *get to one* works. We can infer something important about how God defines faithfulness, and that it involves multiplication. Whatever we are given in time, talents, and treasure, we are expected to multiply.

But why, even in light of that understanding, would the Master call that third servant wicked and lazy? Lazy makes sense, but wicked?

In Greek, the word "wicked" is defined as possessing a serious fault that causes you to be hindered in your productivity. The servant's fault was in the way he perceived his master. Instead of seeing him as someone who would cheer him on as he tried to multiply the gold, as someone who will take what we have to give and multiply it beyond our own power, he was afraid of him.

God gifted us with so much so it would be multiplied, not rot in a grave. Multiplying is an act of faithfulness and trust in Him while maintaining the status quo is lazy and even wicked. It's being unfaithful to the God who gave you everything you have. Fear is what stopped that third servant, what led to him having nothing, what led to him being punished.

We can't treat stewardship lightly. What God gives us, we return back to him, multiplied. We can't plant half a seed and hope for a whole tree. We can't be worried about keeping up with the Joneses. The magic isn't in the money; if you don't do the hard work of rowing upstream and transforming your situation, sometimes more money just gets you more grief.

You have to get to one.

A zero multiplied by any other number is still zero. A negative multiplied by a positive will still be a negative. We have to move to the positive side of that equation and get to one.

What does that look like?

It means living in the present but leading from the future. It means grasping how compounding interest works, and what that means once you get to one. More than 99 percent of Warren Buffet's more than one hundred billion net worth was made after his 50th birthday. Famously, Buffet didn't purchase a new car in his thirties because he could see that every cent past one he made would snowball into compounding growth.

Surround yourself with people who think like Warren Buffet, who think like those first and second servants, people who are on the same mission as you. You want to be in the same boat as people who are willing to row upstream. You need to upgrade your circle.

UPGRADE YOUR CIRCLE

Jim Rohn, an entrepreneur who became a millionaire twice, reduced this final part of the trinity of uncommon freedom into a simple equation, "You are the average of the five people you spend the most time with."

Take a good hard look at the people around you, and ask yourself this question: "Would I want to trade lives with these people?" If the answer is no, you've got to upgrade your circle.

Darren Hardy describes this perfectly with his analogy of the engines vs. anchors. Everyone fits in one category or the other. The people you are surrounding yourself with are either acting as engines or as anchors. Some propel you forward, others hold you back.

A friend of ours went through an extended period of struggle in her life. She was still rowing hard upstream, but to her, it probably felt as if she was getting nowhere. An acquaintance asked her why she kept trying, and why she didn't just give up. Rowing upstream didn't seem valuable.

Arizona friends Robert, Chris, Thomas and Mark talked me into running my first (and only) Tough Mudder. We need friends who challenge us!

There's more than one group of people you can plug yourself into, but our friend chose to build her circle with our group. Though she might not tell you her life is where she wants it, she is contending, she is moving upstream bit by bit, and she's not giving up. We're so proud of her.

I can almost predict someone's success based on how many of the people they surround themselves with choose to take their health journey seriously. Researchers discovered that if your close friend becomes obese, your risk of becoming obese increases by 171 percent. If a sibling becomes obese, your chances of obesity increase by 40 percent. If your spouse gains weight, you're 37 percent more likely to gain weight as well.[3]

A friend told me about a client they worked with who had a goal of being able to bounce on a trampoline with her niece and to go on a mission trip to India with her church family. Before she started working with our friend, she was too heavy to safely bounce on a trampoline, and because of her weight-related medications, she couldn't visit a foreign country because of her need for medical care. Plus, she was embarrassed to take up

3. Friends and Family May Play a Role in Obesity," National Institutes of Health, August 13, 2007, https://www.nih.gov/news-events/nih-research-matters/friends-family-may-play-role-obesity.

two seats and use the seat belt extender in front of a plane full of people.

She had incredible success early on, shedding weight at a fantastic rate. The problem for her came when she began to share her successes with her community. Many were similarly overweight and unhealthy, and instead of cheering her on to meet her goals they started to pull her back down. They were critical of her weight loss and encouraged her to slow down, to take it easy.

She stopped rowing upstream because no one in her boat was rowing with her.

Who's in your boat with you? Are they sitting with their feet up, watching you row, while prodding you to stop, take it easy, and go with the flow instead? The client never recovered from her community's lack of support, and based on photos my friend sees on social media, they doubt this person could jump on a trampoline or take that trip.

Rowing is exponential. When everyone in the boat is rowing, the forward movement greatly increases. The combined momentum makes rowing much easier than if you were the only one rowing in a boat full of people.

When I started my weight loss journey, I was still in my career with the police force. As I mentioned, the police department is not an entirely positive health environment. Dealing with criminal activity and meeting

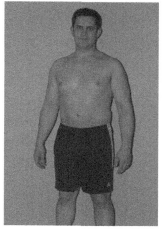
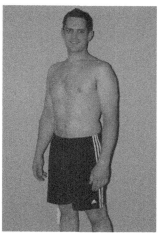

My before and after photo from the 4 week biggest loser competition that was the catalyst for my health journey.

people on the worst day of their lives really grinds at the soul. Health is tossed aside as officers try to find ways to deal with the stress.

My sergeant saw this downward health trend and decided the department should try a weight loss challenge like *The Biggest Loser.* It was only a four-week challenge, but once I got my hands on the oars of fitness, I knew I wanted to continue my growth far beyond that. I also knew I didn't want to gain it all back once the challenge was over like so many of my fellow officers did. Some tried to lure me back to my old ways during our Saturday morning breakfasts before patrol began, waving doughnuts or pancakes my way. Talk about rowing upstream!

Bekah and I had to strengthen our circle and find people who would encourage us in the right direction. I can't count the number of clients and coaches who have completely reversed their health gains due to their lack of positive community. I have no doubt that my incredible community is the number one reason that I'm still healthy.

Getting my health back was my first battle in the war for uncommon freedom, and it will be yours, too. Physical health is the wellspring of energy and possibility that will fuel every other area of your life, whether spiritual, emotional, or financial.

CHAPTER 3

GET YOUR BODY
ON MISSION

God was very specific about how he wanted his Tabernacle to look.

He told Moses down to the smallest detail about the finely woven fabrics, the astounding amounts of gold overlay, the silver, the bronze—just consider how beautiful the actual temple was, once Israel was able to build a permanent house for God.

Today, our bodies are God's temple (1 Corinthians 6:19–20). He made our bodies the most amazing machines on this planet, so complex that we have only begun to understand how they work. This is the home, the vehicle he placed his spirit in, the pinnacle of his creation, and barring illness or injury, it's up to you how you'll enable that vehicle to perform.

You can drive around in a rusted-out station wagon, the actual car of my childhood, or you can get to work and transform it into a sleek Corvette, the dream car of my childhood (or your dream car of choice)!

I wouldn't recommend the old station wagon, because that's what I used to be. By the end of my time in the police force, my body was breaking down on me. My hubcaps were rusty and my bumper wobbled more than I'd like to admit. In truth, I was trapped in a physical body that couldn't do what I wanted or needed it to do. And that sucked.

I injured my back working construction in my twenties, an injury that never fully healed. When I entered the police force, my weight quickly got out of control, and that did nothing to help my back problems. When I turned thirty, I added to the mess by injuring a disk in my back during a softball game. The surgery required after that injury was brutal and invasive, and it took two months to get back to life as usual. Yet sitting for hours in a cop car and lugging around a heavy-duty utility belt only put more pressure on my lower back, and I was pretty sure the next stop would be Repeat Back Surgery City.

I hated the beat-up old station wagon my body had become.

No one can transform your body for you. No one can trade in the old car for a better one except you. Only you can put down the donut and lace up your running shoes. Only you can go against the current. Against the culture of poor health that's everywhere you look.

When you grab onto the power of transformation, the change that happens isn't isolated. It expands into every area of your life. But we live our lives in our physical bodies, so that's why we start with finding uncommon freedom here, first.

GETTING MY HEALTH TO ONE

I remember being trapped in that downstream current, riding closer to severe health issues every day. I'll be forever grateful to Bekah for rowing upstream first.

Bekah upgraded our circle with now-close friends and business mentors, Doug and Thea Wood. They began teaching her the basic habits and mindsets of health they had transformed their lives with. I didn't know it right away, but they were helping us establish the first pillar of uncommon freedom.

And it started over dinner, of all things.

Bekah invited the Woods to our house after they started attending our church again. It was clear they'd made some changes, as they had lost over one hundred pounds together and both radiated positivity and passion. While that dinner wasn't filled with fireworks and a-ha moments that instantly changed me, it was the start of a new season. To be honest, I was pretty skeptical. The typical guy with his arms crossed and an eyebrow raised. But what they said stuck with me.

The following Sunday at church, I started noticing that a bunch of people I knew were dropping pounds fast and looking healthier than ever before. The person who really impressed me was Alex, the soundboard guy, who somehow dropped over one hundred pounds in what seemed like no time at all.

Holy smokes, he melted away! How did I miss that? I remember thinking. I couldn't wrap my head around how I could be so good at observing clues at work, yet miss the hundreds, if not thousands, of pounds that my church friends were losing.

All around us, people were finding healthier versions of themselves, as positive changes spread through our community like wildfire.

In January 2011, after our son Dylan was born, Bekah started her own health journey.

At first, I was a spectator. I watched from the outside while Bekah became healthier. I was still focused on banking as much overtime as I could so we could have a summer vacation. While I was impressed with what Bekah was doing, I was still floating downstream.

A few months later, though, on Wednesday, April 20th, 2011, my friend and Shift Sergeant Alex Oh suggested that our team start a four-week Biggest Loser® competition. I didn't care too much about the health part, but I love a good competition. I was in it to win it. Twelve officers decided to give

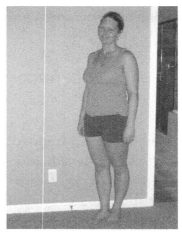

Bekah in January, 2011 at the beginning of her health journey compared to her in 2023, living at around 15% body fat- a very impressive number for any female!

it a try, each of us tossing ten dollars into a pot for a "winner take all" competition. As always, I was motivated to earn some extra cash. Little did Sergeant Oh know that this tiny pebble he was throwing into my life would create a ripple effect that would ultimately lead to me "retiring" from the Hillsboro Police Department a mere twenty-one months later. If there was a "moment of conception" that would lead to the birth of uncommon freedom for me, this was it.

I remembered all the people at church losing weight in addition to my wife, who was looking leaner and hotter by the day, so I immediately knew how I was going to win this competition. When I got home I went to Bekah and got on board with the program. She was pretty excited that I was starting my own health journey, though the reality is that I had what I'd call a "diet mentality." That is, I just wanted to shed weight to earn a reward at the end. I wasn't thinking about lifestyle change.

Our competition started on Saturday, April 23, 2011. In fact, on my way to the central precinct on weigh-in day I drove out of my way to swing by a donut shop so I could devour a few more donuts just to tip the scale a bit further to make my glorious victory all the better. Plus, in true diet mentality, I felt like these donuts were going to be my "last meal," at least for a while. Maybe I started a little off-target. After following Jesus and marrying Bekah, this was one of the most life-altering decisions I ever made. Because choosing to get healthy is the rising tide that lifts all our boats.

WHY OPTIMIZE HEALTH?

What activity is there that being unhealthy would help you perform better?

None.

Optimizing your health means not living in a diet mentality but embracing a new lifestyle, one that will serve you for the rest of your life—and actually allow you to *live* your life to the fullest. As I mentioned before, research shows that if a spouse or close friend becomes obese, you're much more likely to do the same. On the other hand, if you get healthy with another person close to you, you're more likely to succeed and stay there. The principle of anchors and engines applies.

As a father, I realized that being unhealthy had a negative impact on my family.

Your level of health will create the launchpad for your child's health. Dr. Manish Motwanie, a senior obesity surgeon, recently conducted a study and found, "A child with one or both obese parents will have an 80 percent chance of being obese."[4] Consider that when Bekah started eating healthier, she made healthier foods for the whole family. Her pursuit of health had a trickle-down effect on the entire family.

Being unhealthy limited what I could do with my kids. According to the Exchange Family Center, playing together is one of the most effective tools for building a strong relationship with your child, especially when they are young. Many of their formative memories are made in those years. Playing with your kids builds trust, resilience, and joy in your relationship. Plus, when parents play with their kids, oxytocin is released and that makes you feel good, too!

Had a bad day? Go play.

You can't do any of that if you're not healthy enough to move, though. When your body is a broken-down vehicle, you're missing out on building important relationships in your family.

---

4. Longjam Dineshwori, "Obese Parents Are Likely to Have Obese or Overweight Children: Study," The Health Site, April 19, 2021, https://www.thehealthsite.com/diseasesconditions/obesity/obese-parents-are-likely-to-have-obese-or-overweight-childrenstudy-888665/.

Watching your kids play from the sidelines isn't the same. I love the times I get to play basketball or football with my kids. I can only do that because I lost the extra weight and keep rowing to improve my health. At age seventy-four, Bekah's dad, who was one of her first health coaching clients, is still active and able to play with his grandkids.

Bekah's dad Roger with Evie on our trampoline.

Optimizing our health has allowed us to participate in mission trips, improve family dynamics, and experience new activities. It has also improved our emotional, mental, and spiritual lives. A body in pain or functioning poorly is louder than any other input and affects all output.

It's not a hard sell, convincing people to optimize their health. The tricky part is the pitfalls in your way.

RAPIDS, WHIRLPOOLS, AND HIDDEN DANGERS AHEAD

A health journey is exactly that, a journey. It's not a destination that you arrive at and settle in for good. And like laundry, it's never done.

We're all fighting aging, and the further we get upstream reduces how far we'll drift downstream as we get older.

There wasn't a lightning bolt moment where I changed forever. We all ask God to wave his cosmic wand and change us instantaneously, but for most of us, change comes inch by inch, one step at a time. As the Apostle Paul said in Hebrews 12:1-2, this is about endurance and contending to the end. Most of us have a thorn in the flesh that we contend with every day. But its presence (and the daily struggle) doesn't mean we're failing. It means we're human.

Consider an anchor on the end of a chain. We want to cut the chain and ditch the anchor in a single stroke.

And we can.

Break a link, and we can shed the anchor.

But if we don't break the right link, we're still dragging around a heavy chain.

There's a collective weight in the things that hold us back, all those little habits that end up being as heavy as the anchor itself. Overspending, porn, drinking too much alcohol, yelling at our kids—it's great if we can break one of these links, but too many of us break a link and then go fishing for the anchor to reattach it to the shorter chain. Or we add a link after we've broken it, not realizing the longer chain creates more drag force.

You can't move with the anchor in the ground, but you make rowing upstream difficult if you're dragging heavy chains. We have to get rid of the anchor *and* the chain entirely, whether link by link or finding that one link that's holding all the weight.

Every day you contend, you break a link. But if you're unwilling to chip away at the links, you're not ready to change your lifestyle. You're only on a diet for a while. Or a workout kick temporarily. Or a quit-smoking process for a week or two.

Please understand, I'm not pretending change in these areas isn't damn hard. Because it is. But uncommon freedom in our health doesn't come with an escalator.

We all get tired. We all have times when we slow down or even drift back a bit. I get it because I've had plenty. Life erupts with storms and it saps our energy. When that happens, will you quit or pick up the oars again? Will you break that anchor chain one link at a time?

Now, allow me to predict your future: there are obstacles ahead that will make your journey difficult. In my experience, three obstacles in particular do more damage to people on their health journey than anything else.

ANCHOR 1: THE HOUSE ALWAYS WINS

Modern food isn't here to help you live your best life. In fact, it's barely food at all.

It was carefully designed to be addictive, using packaging and ingredients that we can't resist unless we're aggressively rowing upstream. Millions of dollars are poured into marketing agencies to trick us into choosing options that destroy our health. Did you know sugar is more addictive than cocaine?[5] I contend against my sugar addiction on a daily basis, frequently losing battles. I just refuse to lose the war.

Colors are weaponized and used to entice us to choose cheap, disease-inducing products. Brands use red and yellow in their packaging because these colors have been scientifically proven to heighten nerve impulses and increase heart rate, which mimics our brain chemistry when we are hungry.[6] The color yellow is processed by the brain faster than any other color, so it grabs your attention quickly, even releasing a small amount of serotonin when you look at it.

Advertisers are using your own body chemistry against you. We're at the poker table of life nurturing false hope, because the

5. "Is Sugar More Addictive Than Cocaine," New Hall Hospital, September 20, 2017, https://www.newhallhospital.co.uk/news/is-sugar-more-addictive-than-cocaine.
6. "How Food Packaging Color Influences Consumer Behavior," Hart Design, April 12, 2016, https://hartdesign.com/industry-news/food-packagingcolor-influences-consumer-behavior/.

house always wins. Not only that, but we have allowed food to do too much work for us, work it was never intended to do.

As a police officer, riding around in my patrol car was hours of boredom interrupted by moments of sheer terror. I got into the habit of basically eating a box of candy on every shift because I used eating to combat boredom and stay alert. To this day, when I'm in the car I want to snack. Now I bring along sunflower seeds or something healthy. I know the car triggers me and this is how I contend with that habit.

Habits, triggers, routines—they can all stall you out in your health journey.

Habits are often burrowed deep into the subconscious. We're not always aware of the habit, and even if we are, we don't always know why we're doing it. We need to do an audit and ask ourselves what job we are asking these unhealthy habits to do for us.

Emotional eater? Food is doing the work of comforting anxiety.

Bored? Food is giving you stimulation.

Use treats to reward? Food is keeping you from showing love in better ways.

I've often said that we have a strange romantic relationship with food. When we're happy, we eat. When we're sad, we eat. When we feel out of control, we eat (or starve ourselves). There's the old saying that we should eat to live, not live to eat. We're asking food to do what it wasn't meant to do; we have to break up that relationship and instead think of food as fuel. When you take a road trip, do you stop at every gas station on the way to fill up? Some of us do that with food. Do you wait for your gas tank to get down to fumes and then fuel up? Some of us do that with food.

But the current carrying you downstream wants you to use food for everything but fuel. We are told that a happy meal will make us happy, energy drinks give us energy, and Snickers will solve the problem of being hangry. If we're just floating along downstream, we're not aware of these lies. We'll find ourselves waking up to rampant inflammation in our bodies, brain fog sapping away our potential.

Today, the game of food is rigged.

It was designed to keep you hooked.

Riding the current, when it comes to health and the lies you're being fed, is a deadly gamble. The house always wins unless you stop playing their game.

ANCHOR 2: YOU'RE IN THE WRONG CIRCLE

There is no normal, there's just familiarity.

What's around us the most is what becomes normal to us. Once that baseline is established, we compare ourselves to that to know whether or not we're within the right parameters.

That's dangerous if you've surrounded yourself with the wrong circle of people.

I hate to say it, but the most powerful roadblock to optimal health is your immediate circle of family and friends. You'll rise or fall to the level of what's around you. People will either be your anchor or your engine. Think of the holiday when you showed up and your family pressured you to eat food you know isn't healthy, or how they became upset with you because they equated food with family and happiness.

Family and friends aren't the only things you're surrounded by. Media and advertising are part of your circle, too. For decades, advertising normalized ultra-skinny physiques, especially in women. The 1990s in particular was an era of models who were unhealthily skinny. Now we're seeing the opposite, where obesity is glorified and normalized on screens and in clothing stores. Both extremes have an effect on real life ranging from eating disorders to increasing obesity rates.

Another advertising moniker that I can't stand is the "dad bod." Stores are now selling t-shirts that are tight at the arms and chest and loose in the gut, to make men look bigger where they want to and to hide their big bellies. Who ever said dads are supposed to be fat? Why is a "dad bod" something that now equates to having a big stomach?

The media you consume is part of your circle.

It's not easy, I know. But you have to decide not to let others, whether it's a family friend, advertising, or a reality TV show, tell you what to eat or how to be healthy.

Remember my friend's client who got lost on her journey to health because her friends sidetracked her and had her drop an anchor where she was? I see this over and over again, people rowing upstream only to stop because they surrounded themselves with the wrong community. I can't tell you how sad it is to see clients and coaches who had success, only to let it go and start back downstream again. They listened to people who said they'd done enough, that where they were was good enough.

I'm not successful because I'm perfect. In fact, I struggle with a sugar addiction, and there are moments where I've binged on junk over the years.

I'm a health coach and I'm eating this crap, I would think, feeling guilt. Honestly, as I write this book I'm coming off a short season where I once again over-consumed junk food. I'm getting back on track by publicly declaring my commitment to fast from junk food until my body fat is back under 10 percent.

When we fail, it's easy to think we're not worthy. I've seen it paralyze people to the point of keeping them from even starting their health journey.

"I can't be perfect, so I'm not even going to start," they say.

The enemy likes to tell us two lies: we've done enough, or we've not done enough. We're perfect, or we'll never be perfect.

Whichever hooks our personality best gets weaponized. Both send us downstream eventually.

I don't have ironclad will, but I do have a great community. I have people intent on upgrading their lives and pursuing uncommon freedom. I have my health coach and a personal trainer. I've been a part of a great group at a fitness gym (although my current preferred gym is in my garage).

My Oregon friends David and Matt chose to get healthy with me back in 2011.

Being healthy means I get to play in father/son Turkey Bowl football games instead of watching from the sidelines!

I have my wife, Bekah. When I struggle, she makes sure I keep the oars in the water. I do the same to encourage her. It's rare that we both get off track at the same time unless we make a conscious decision to splurge for a special occasion or a trip. Even then, we have a plan to resume rowing upstream as soon as possible.

We're all rowing toward excellence, upstream, encouraging each other through our weaknesses, and never allowing each other to drop an anchor. There's no one in my boat who isn't rowing.

While I want to be a great example and inspire others toward health, I have to be careful that I don't let the influence go in the wrong direction. You inherit what you surround yourself with, whether that's success or failure. You can encourage your friends to get in your boat and row with you, but you can't get in their boat and expect to change their direction.

Community matters. What kind of community have you surrounded yourself with? Does it help you row, or encourage you to go downstream?

ANCHOR 3: LETTING DOWNSTREAM PEOPLE TELL YOU THAT YOU'RE A SUCCESS

This obstacle may sound harsh, but let me explain: If you're pursuing excellence in an area, why would you allow someone who has failed (or not achieved that same excellence) tell you how you're doing? They can't possibly know. It's not a judgment against them as a person. Instead, where their life is in that area is a clue about which voices you might want to listen to, and which you might want to tune out altogether. Never let someone uninterested in their health tell you that you're taking your own health too seriously. That's as foolish as taking financial advice from a broke person!

People who are floating downstream are only going to influence you to row less. You can't allow yourself to operate by their standards. No one should set your standards but you or the people you would trade places with.

Someone who is overweight should not be telling you, *you're skinny enough*. Someone who is in financial ruin should not be saying, you have enough money. An unhealthy person saying you're doing great when you're only halfway to your goal might cause you to stop the journey.

Not all cheering is created equal. Some voices cause confusion. Some cause you to slow down. Some cause you to drop an anchor and hang out because you're in a pretty good place. Only the right voices will propel the right choices. Be careful who you listen to.

MUSCULAR CHRISTIANITY

When Charles Spurgeon, who liked to smoke cigars, gave a talk on the benefits of moderation, it wasn't long until someone called him out. How would he define moderation, in terms of his cigar smoking, they wondered?

"One at a time," Spurgeon replied.

In church, we have a tendency to push physical health off to the side as less important. But we are made of three parts: body, spirit, and soul.

Sometimes I get pushback for focusing on physical health, but all three parts are interconnected. We can't separate our physical body from our spiritual nature. One is not more beloved by our Creator than the other. Someday, we'll all be resurrected into physical bodies. Sins against the body, whether sexual or gluttony, are sins. It's clear that for God, the physical matters, too. Otherwise, we'd all be floating around as wispy spirits.

We've seen thousands of clients whose spiritual and mental health improved when their physical health improved. We've also seen people whose lack of physical health has kept them in emotional and spiritual bondage. We are integrated; if one part is unhealthy, it affects the rest.

In the late 1800s and early 1900s, a movement began that connected improved fitness and health as part of Christian discipleship.[7] The idea was that strengthening physical bodies would help push church culture in a direction of action. It would cultivate great resilience in the face of challenges. And, in general, it would encourage a more vigorous approach to life instead of

7. Brett McKay and Kate McKay, "When Christianity Was Muscular," The Art of Manliness, https://hartdesign.com/industry-news/food-packagingcolor-influences-consumer-behavior/.

WE CAN'T SEPARATE
OUR PHYSICAL
BODY FROM OUR
SPIRITUAL NATURE.
ONE IS NOT MORE
BELOVED BY
OUR CREATOR
THAN THE OTHER.

sedentary passivity. They believed that a follower of Jesus could not afford to ignore or mistreat his body, and that physical health could either be a great aid or a significant hindrance to living the gospel.

In 2011, Gary Thomas wrote *Every Body Matters: Strengthening Your Body to Strengthen Your Soul*. In his book, he made the same connection between a healthy body and a healthy spirit. A weak and unhealthy body can make a person prone to complaining and excess, finding comfort in passive entertainment.

It's a downstream way of living, and, as Thomas notes, it creates souls that are "all but irrelevant in kingdom warfare. They are no threat to anyone—least of all to Satan."

"In the end, I found that physical fitness offered to God, surrendered to God, pursued in cooperation with God has enormous spiritual, emotional, and physical benefits," Thomas wrote.

Barring injury or disease, there is no reason to let physical weakness or weariness keep you from giving those around you a full life, whether it's your family, your spouse, your church, or your community. Being at a healthy weight *and* being active is the key. This combination is the 20 percent that makes 80 percent of the difference.

It's one thing to reach a healthy weight, it's another thing to keep improving.
Bekah and I are both the healthiest we've ever been in our 40s and invite our kids
(here my son Dylan) to join us in the gym.

What a shame to have to say no to God because we're physically unable to go. What a shame to have a spirit and soul housed in a body that cannot give God the full service he intended when he uniquely designed us with the capability of reaching our full potential.

Do you want to live life more abundantly? To live your faith vigorously? To be in a position to help others and do the work that needs to be done?

Get your body on mission and watch how every key life area improves. As surprising as it sounds, the same principles set up your finances to thrive.

CHAPTER 4

MASTER YOURSELF, MASTER YOUR WEALTH

What if every time you went fishing, you got a little bit richer?

As a hobby, fishing tends to eat up money, not generate it, but we read of a miracle in which God caused coins to show up out of nowhere in a fish's mouth (Matthew 17:27). Great way to earn a living.

Building wealth is about luck and miracles, right? The right bait, the right moment, the right fish, and boom. Gold coins.

Wrong.

God absolutely can make something out of nothing. It's how he made everything in the universe. But thinking of miracles only in those terms sets us up for failure. More often than not, a "miracle" is because people have been faithful and good stewards of whatever God has blessed them with. They've been obedient to him. They heard God's command and went out to do the work.

What if there's a coin in every fish, but we're too lazy to get the fish?

AVERAGE FINANCES, ABOVE AVERAGE STRESS

In 2019, the average American family had a median net worth (total assets minus total liabilities) of just over $120,000.[8] Census data showed that the real median household income in the U.S. in 2021 was about $70,000.[9] The numbers are lower for younger age groups.

Essentially, the average person is living paycheck to paycheck. They're not going to get ahead, relying on savings and Social

8. Neil Bhutta et. al. "Changes in U.S. Family Finances from 2016 to 2019: Evidence from the Survey of Consumer Finances," Federal Reserve Board, September 2020, https://www.federalreserve.gov/publications/files/scf20.pdf.
9. Jessica Semega and Melissa Kollar, "Income and Poverty in the United States: 2021," United States Census Bureau, September 13, 2022, https://www.census.gov/library/publications/2022/demo/p60-276.html.

Security with a retirement looming that will force them to live off much less than they did during their working years. And considering the path we're on, the dollar is going to be worth much less by then.

People stuck in the average state of finances aren't giving much, if at all. Giving is based on what's left over at the end of the month instead of prioritizing giving at the front end of the month.

Average people have a lot of debt, and they get through life financing nearly everything or having to say no to things due to financial strain. The average American's entire lifestyle is governed by lack of finances, even though we live in the wealthiest nation in the world. Health decisions are based on insurance coverage instead of what's best for your health. Opportunities for your kids are based on what you can afford instead of what's best for them. You have to take every overtime hour offered, whether you want to or not. When the average person takes a vacation, they put it on credit cards and end up more stressed when they come home.

You can vacation on a budget!

Being financially stuck means lots of fights over finances, no matter what level of wealth you are at. Being wealthy doesn't mean you can do a poor job managing that wealth. Maybe your net worth is decreasing, which is a real problem when you've made money your idol and connected your personal worth as a human to your net worth in the bank. Maybe massive, crushing debt is causing you anxiety. Maybe you think happiness is tied to the idea that if you could make X amount of money, your problems will go away.

Someone who is stuck has few choices. Their life is driven by financial decisions, needing to earn money whether for actual needs or chasing after happiness through gambling and shopping addictions that make you feel momentary joy before crashing into anxiety. Getting you dopamine hits from spending is a terrible problem.

Uncommon freedom in finances creates people who have a very different relationship with money. Instead of the "shirtsleeves to shirtsleeves in three generations" pattern, in which a family's wealth is lost by the grandkids who felt entitled to it, something different is at work.

Uncommon freedom isn't about making a pile of cash. It starts earlier, in how you view money and the decisions you make around it, whether you have lots of cash or not.

What does it look like?

You're actively giving with ridiculous generosity, making a significant impact. Your only debt is your mortgage, and it's reasonable (25 percent or less of your income). You have an emergency fund of three to six months of living expenses. You're saving for retirement in a way that you take ownership over your own retirement, not relying on Social Security and not being chained to a job you don't like, just hoping that they don't fire you before you qualify for their retirement or pension. Your net worth increases each year. You make medical decisions based on what's best for you, not by what you can afford or what your insurance plan dictates as the standard of care. Vacations aren't a way to escape from everyday life, because your everyday life is something you enjoy living.

Uncommon freedom is where you control your money. It doesn't control you.

UNCOMMON FREEDOM
IS WHERE YOU
CONTROL YOUR
MONEY. IT DOESN'T
CONTROL YOU.

Money isn't a zero-sum game, where we have to chase after the biggest slice of the pie. Uncommon freedom realizes you can keep making more pies, and more pies for you doesn't mean fewer pies for everyone else.

When it comes to money, having uncommon freedom is an entire mindset shift.

If you need help shifting your mind on how you think about your current wealth, consider that nearly half of the world lives on less than $5.50 a day.[10] If you are above that standard, you've already won the lottery when it comes to finances. There's a website where you can see for yourself how you rank in the world.[11]

While it's great to get perspective, though, how do you move from stuck or average toward uncommon financial freedom? Knowing you're in the top percent for wealth around the world isn't going to help you pay down your credit card debt. It isn't going to help you if you're stuck in a job where you look forward to Fridays and dread Sunday nights.

If you hate your job, if your spouse or family hate your job, if you're not being challenged at your job, if your job isn't supporting your spending or allowing you to live the life you want—it's time to redesign your financial lifestyle.

FOUR STEPS TOWARD UNCOMMON FINANCIAL FREEDOM

"Many quit just short of the breakthrough," author John Bevere writes in his book *X: Multiply Your God-Given Potential.*

10. Kate Gibson, "Nearly Half the Planet's Population Lives on Less Than $5.50 a Day," CBS News, October 17, 2018, https://www.cbsnews.com/news/nearly-half-the-planets-populationlives-on-less-than-5-50-a-day-worlf-bank-reports/.
11. https://web.archive.org/web/20191229104608/http://www.globalrichlist.com/wealth.

"They've been overwhelmed by adversity or the lack of desired results."

Think of the cartoon of a man digging for gold. He's dug a deep hole so far, the ground towering above his head, his shovel worn thin. But he's chosen to give up because it seems obvious to him there's no gold to be found. Yet we see, in the cartoon, that there's gold just an inch below where he chose to stop.

Getting to uncommon freedom in your finances doesn't happen overnight. It takes time and perseverance. But here are some steps you can take now that will build on each other. They'll get you there much more quickly than you'd imagined.

Bekah and I have been controlled by the need to make every last dollar no matter how many hours of overtime I had to put in. I get how hard it can be. But we followed four basic steps toward uncommon freedom in our finances. And we know, from experience, that these steps work.

GET OUT OF DEBT

The first thing to do in your move toward uncommon freedom in your finances is to stop spending money you don't have.

Stop it right now. It's only putting you further in debt.

We live in a credit-fueled culture where buying now and paying later (and paying interest forever, never touching principal) is completely normal. There's no delay in gratification. You're told that if you want it, get it now and deal with the fallout later. The problem is that when you use tomorrow to get what you want today, that's financial enslavement, not freedom. Debt is the enemy and we've grown completely comfortable with that enemy sitting at the table and eating tomorrow's dinner.

This isn't something reserved for those with lower incomes. For most people, when their income increases so does their debt. They think they have to match their standard of living with every income increase, and they'll never have enough money because they haven't understood this first and most important principle: You have to stop going into debt, no matter what your income is.

GET RID OF WHAT YOU CAN'T AFFORD

The next thing you need to do is get rid of things you can't afford.

This will be tough because a lot of the things we can't afford we rely on to give us happiness and meaning on days that otherwise feel like drudgery. When we have a wrong relationship with money, we chase after things we can't afford and ask them to be a substitute for real relationships and faith.

That could be subscriptions, television streaming services, vehicles with high insurance, or full-time college tuition—if you can't afford to keep it, get rid of it. Find a way to reduce those costs.

My youngest brother, Scott, graduated from college debt-free. He went to a community college, then a local public university, and he applied for scholarships like it was his full-time job. He still worked to pay for some expenses, but he came away with no student loans! There are tons of scholarships available for those who are willing to put in the effort to find them.

Don't finance things at all, if possible.

I'm not a financial advisor giving out professional advice, but what I've learned from experience is that you shouldn't finance anything other than your home. It's always tempting to finance something. During the COVID-19 pandemic, our family started chartering flights to avoid the massive headaches of commercial travel. It was extremely expensive and we began investigating the possibility of purchasing our own aircraft. During that time, I had a conversation with one of my best friends from high school, Kris. He is financially savvy and also happens to have multiple ratings as a pilot. When I asked him about financing a jet he asked me, "Would you finance a charter trip?" The obvious answer was, "Absolutely not!"

That was all it took for me to remember to live by the principles I preach. Even now I catch myself thinking about why it would make sense to own something, instead of renting or chartering, knowing it would take financing to achieve that. I have to remind myself that, generally, if I have to finance something, it means I can't afford it. In 2023, when our business took a 25 percent hit in revenue, I was very glad I stuck to my principles on this.

That's part of the debt piece mentioned earlier, but financing is offered everywhere. When you look at the cost of a car or couch that's purchased through financing, the cost is much higher than the original price tag and puts what might be affordable at first glance into the unaffordable range. You can't afford to be paying money to borrow money.

Use your library for books and videos. Shop secondhand. Go to college part-time or go to a community college if you can. Be content with the possessions you have, if they're functional and working. Don't try to keep up with the Joneses (because they're probably in debt anyway). Go camping nearby instead of flying the family to Hawaii.

Like Dave Ramsey says, "If you live like no one else now, later you can live and give like no one else." When Bekah and I decided we were going to live without debt, we knew we'd have to sacrifice. We were the couple with one fully-paid-for used car. We had a single twenty-seven-inch tube television, while everyone we knew had multiple big screens.

We only owned used cars until we purchased our first brand new car in 2019, a scarlet red F-150. The smell of a new car is so much better when you aren't making payments on it!

We were the ones who didn't order drinks at restaurants because they were out of our budget. But now that we're living like no one else, those sacrifices seem more than worth it, and I would do it exactly the same given the chance again.

Remember, you're working your way toward uncommon financial freedom. When you get there, some of these things will be back in your life but without the debt and burden they have now.

USE CASH AND TRACK YOUR SPENDING

Pay cash for as much as you're able.

Not every situation will allow for it, but make the effort to use cash when possible. I'm not a hardline "never use a credit card" guy because we appreciate the great rewards you can get from some cards. However, if you can't pay your card balance off every month, then use cash. Get rid of your cards except one for emergencies. And *never* pay interest on credit card debt.

Part of using cash is paying attention to how you're using your money. Track your money and expenses, whatever form of money you're using, because tracking creates an awareness of what you're doing. That's true whether you track your food, your exercise, or your finances.

Pay attention to the habits you want to get rid of and the ones you want to create. You won't magically transform into a person who saves your money once you hit six figures. You become that person long before then because the habit is what helps you get there.

LEVERAGE YOUR TIME INSTEAD OF TRADING IT

Finally, figure out how you can make more money by leveraging your time, not just trading your time.

A lever is a simple device that lets you move more weight with less power if it's used correctly.

Know what your time is worth. Figure out what you make, and then evaluate that compared to the other things you do. What could you delegate and pay someone to do to free up more time? Would that cost make sense in terms of what your time is worth and your potential ability to make more money if you had more time?

Let's say you make fifty dollars an hour, and you have the ability to work more if you need or want to. It makes sense to pay someone twenty dollars an hour to do something you don't enjoy, something that takes up your time and keeps you from working another fifty-dollar hour. You're still making thirty dollars an hour, and you're getting ahead.

If you don't believe me, let me tell you about the two thousand dollar oil change.

I know some people who insist on changing the oil in their vehicles themselves. There's nothing wrong with that, but it's a hassle, and there are shops you could go to for that same service where they take care of the headache (including the collection and disposal of the old oil). But we have the idea that doing it yourself can save money.

And it's true, it can save money, except for that one time when the oil filter doesn't get put on properly.

In this particular instance, the filter fell off, the oil leaked out, the engine froze, and over two thousand dollars had to be spent on a new engine. That was an expensive attempt at saving money, not to mention the time it took. Few things cause more headaches, cursing, and fighting than trying to save a few bucks to do something yourself instead of hiring someone who's good at doing the job.

When living in Okinawa, at first I was amazed at how small the houses were. There wasn't space for a garage full of tools and equipment. But I quickly saw that this wasn't a problem; it was a thing of genius. When they needed something done, they paid a professional. Instead of spending time and money on buying and maintaining tools, the professional took care of it. And if anything went wrong, the professional carried the liability. What a concept!

In Robert T. Kiyosaki's book *The Cashflow Quadrant*, he tells readers how to move beyond "job security" (i.e., trading time for money) to financial freedom (making leverage work for you). He tells the story of a father and sons who have a business that requires them to get buckets of water every day. A competitor came along and instead of using buckets, built a pipe. The answer wasn't to get more buckets but to build something different. You have to move to a different quadrant.

Be sure you pick the right quadrant.

I know of people who have great ideas and start a business from scratch with a ton of overhead, and then find that the time, start-up costs, and regulations choke out any path to prosperity. A side hustle that has a big overhead cost won't help you with leverage.

On the other hand, as Kiyosaki points out, you won't grow wealth if you don't have a business because you're missing out on tax write-offs and deductions. I'm not giving you tax advice, but starting a home business or a side hustle without huge start-up costs is a great idea for a lot of reasons.

Remember the movie *Tommy Boy*? Their sales trip was a disaster; they sold nothing and it was one debacle after another. Yet that whole horrific trip was a write-off. If only Clark Griswold had an LLC.

Without leverage and its compounding effect (which we'll talk about in a bit), you won't increase your wealth because you're simply trading time for dollars in an equal exchange. You won't find yourself moving into new circles of association that can help you compound your investment even more by opening up new opportunities. Opportunities orbit people, and people with uncommon freedom have more opportunities around them. We all have the same amount of "luck" but it depends on what you do and who you're around. It requires an understanding of the importance of leverage.

PROSPERITY WITH A PURPOSE

Be the Christian George Soros.

Seriously.

A lot of wealthy people use their money primarily for their own pleasure and enjoyment. It never goes beyond selfishness. If only more would use their money for good.

God rewards us with blessings, and the multiplication principle can be seen throughout scripture. But are we working to multiply those rewards for our own benefit, or to have a godly impact on the world and make it a better place? Considering the multiplication principle and the mandate to do God's work, it's clear we have a moral obligation to increase our wealth in order to use it to do good. I love how Rabbi Daniel Lapin put it in *Business Secrets from the Bible:* "Money is the consequence of doing the right things."

When the Israelites were set free from slavery in Egypt, they plundered the land. God blessed them with all of that plunder because he knew down the road it would be used for worship and for the Tabernacle. Yet before it was ever used for what God intended, the Israelites used it to create a golden calf. They took the blessing and made a literal idol out of it.

Prosperity following God's intent looks very different from prosperity that's become an idol. God blessed Job, Abraham, Jacob, David, Solomon, and many more people throughout the pages of scripture with incredible prosperity. His intention for the Israelites was the Promised Land, a place of his blessing, not slavery to other nations. His intention for us, ultimately, isn't a miserable eternity, but one of never-ending joy and delight.

God is not against prosperity in this life as long as we remember that the point of it isn't just to have a comfortable, pleasurable life, but to multiply the good things. Comfortable lives aren't wrong, mind you. I have a comfortable life, but I make sure that a lot of people benefit from it.

We give to ministries and good causes. We pay people to provide services, like landscaping, home repairs, laundry, and housekeeping because that feeds the economy and makes it possible for the people we hire to have a successful business of their own. When we delegate that work to someone else, we leverage our time and make it possible for them to provide for their families so they can pay it forward. When our employees have earned a raise we give it to them without them having to ask. We've had these principles at work for a while, even when our income wasn't where it is today.

The well dedication in Kenya.

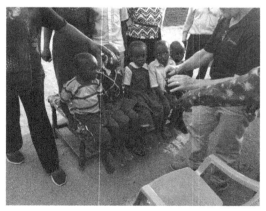
Handing out shoes to the students at the school that was nearest to the well.

Jealousy and envy can get in the way of viewing prosperity with a purpose.

There's always someone who has more than we do. You might be riding on a great yacht, but someone somewhere has another one that's bigger and better. You might have given a big donation only to find out that it was a pittance compared to someone else's. It's like being thirsty and taking a big gulp of seawater only to find yourself more thirsty than before.

Prosperity with a purpose is not a game of comparison, especially when viewed with an understanding of how God rewards and uses obedience. It's not reserved for the super wealthy. It's for everyone. Wherever you're at on the river, if you're rowing upstream, you can live a life of prosperity with a purpose because the long game stretches ahead of you.

SEEING THE LONG GAME

Our kids are given a monthly stipend. They are responsible for managing their own bank accounts (with our guidance and supervision) and use that money to buy things like clothes or their school uniforms on their own. My son was online, buying pants, when he saw something that caught his attention.

"Dad, did you know you can make payments on pants?" he asked, a little surprised.

As the economy tightens, the "buy now, pay later" model has grown increasingly popular.[12] You can find it on nearly every online shopping site for nearly every item imaginable. My son noticed it in the shopping cart for a basic pair of pants.

Seems crazy, doesn't it? Making payments on a pair of khakis.

But the truth is, a lot of people are making payments on pants. They just don't realize it, because that reality is hidden in their credit card debt. They're making payments on pants, on Starbucks coffee from a couple of months ago, on groceries—if it went on the card, they're making payments on it.

---

12 Alicia Wallace, "Red Flag: Consumers Are Using Buy Now, Pay Later to Cover Everyday Expenses," last modified July 6, 2022, https://www.cnn.com/2022/07/06/economy/buy-now-pay-later-bnpl-inflationdata/index.html.

When it comes to taking consumers' money, every point of friction has been erased. Put it on credit, buy now and pay later, so you can have it right now!

When it comes to our finances, most people don't see the long game.

In his brilliant book, *The Psychology of Money*, author Morgan Housel explained what happens when you zoom out and see the bigger picture. Warren Buffett began investing when he was ten years old, and by the time he was thirty-seven, had ten million to his name. And as we know, today he is worth over one hundred billion.

What if Buffett had been spending like a normal person in his teens and twenties? What if he'd been traveling and trying to find out what he loved to do in life? A normal person saves about thirty-five thousand dollars by age thirty. Perhaps then, let's imagine he settled down and started investing seriously, and then quit at age sixty to retire like everyone else. Instead of being worth over one hundred billion, he'd be worth around eleven million today.

Buffett is great with investing, but his real secret is time. He understood the long game.

The Bible tells us to steward what God's given us by investing it wisely (Matthew 25:14-30). This goes for everything, whether that's in finances, health, or relationships.

You don't stop.

You don't bury anything you could be investing. That includes your time, your talent, and your treasure. If you're no longer earning or multiplying when you could be, you're burying. If you're spending money but not giving it, you're burying it. If you're using all your time for yourself instead of putting it toward others, you're burying it.

Burying doesn't multiply, only investing does.

THE COMPOUND EFFECT

Just like relationships where you have to put in intentional effort instead of letting them happen on their own (because worthwhile upstream things just don't happen on their own), we've taken the same approach with our finances and giving.

One of the reasons for taking this approach is that it contrasts with today's world in which you don't have to be great; being good stands out as enough. No need to get too crazy with your faith and boldness. Good isn't thinking out of the box, but it's good enough. Good doesn't blow your mind with service, but it's good enough. The pursuit of excellence almost seems crazy in our culture.

Do you want to compound something that's good or something that's great?

Just remember that whether you're trying to work your way toward uncommon financial freedom or whether you're leveling up when it comes to giving, the compound effect works both ways. Small, consistent activity, whether paying down debt or donating to worthy causes, leads to significant outcomes.

Imagine what would happen if everyone gave at least 10 percent. What if that snowballed? What would it take to get it to snowball?

Take a look at our tithing numbers from the last nine years for an example of this compound effect over time:

- In 2015, we tithed 10 percent of our net personal income.
- In 2016, we tithed 10 percent of our net business income. Our annual net income increase after tithe was 67 percent.
- In 2017, we tithed 10 percent of our gross business revenue. Our annual net income increase after tithe was 47 percent.
- In 2018, we tithed 15 percent of our gross business revenue Our annual net income increase after tithe was 74 percent.
- In 2019, we tithed 20 percent of our gross business revenue. Our annual net income increase after tithe was 39 percent.

In 2020, we tithed 25 percent of our gross business revenue. Our annual net income increase after tithe was 20 percent.

In 2021, we tithed 30 percent of our gross business revenue. Our annual net income increase after tithe was 22 percent.

In 2022, we tithed 35 percent of our gross business revenue. Our annual net income after tithe decreased by less than 4 percent.

Should read: In 2023, we decided to tithe 10 percent of our *desired* gross business revenue, which is a 63 percent increase over 2022, plus we are tithing 30 percent of our actual gross income. It's been a tough year financially, so we are projecting our income to be down about 26 percent. With the decrease in our income and the increase in our tithing, our actual tithe is about 49 percent so far.

Recall that David wanted to build the temple, but God said no because he had blood on his hands. David's son would get to build the temple. So David gave his whole net worth (about four billion dollars) and he did it publicly. When the leaders of the tribes saw his example, they gave, too. It's the heart that *wants* to be seen that doesn't get blessed; there are times when giving publicly can be genuinely from the heart, and because it's public it will inspire others to give, too.

We were approached by a friend to partner with a ministry by giving money to help build a well in Africa. Instead of having him run around trying to find lots of donors, we felt God leading us to not just donate some but to cover the cost of the entire well. Because of that, our entire family was invited to Kenya to be there when they dedicated the well, where all the community leaders turned out. We made a mission trip out of it, and our kids were able to experience what giving does at a whole different level. We were able to visit a nearby school and village that were about a mile from the closest well. We asked what it would take to run pipes from the closest well to the school so the kids could have fresh, clean water. We got the price, funded the project, and now the school has clean water.

Uncommon financial freedom means you aren't limited to giving in small amounts (though there's nothing wrong with that), but that you are able to give to something in its entirety to help make things happen.

An accumulation effect is at work here. Whether it's your bank account, your health, or your relationships, the key is that you need to get started today.

Right now.

Start small, be consistent, and work the plan. You'll see the effect in time because consistency has power.

PROVISION IS ABOUT VISION

This question of uncommon financial freedom is about provision, which, at its root, is about vision.

It's about looking ahead for your family and the legacy that follows, making it about much more than money. It's about practical things of planning, storing up for hard times, giving generously, and creating an all-encompassing lifestyle in which your relationship with money is healthy, neither letting it become an idol nor a master.

Provision is about obedience to God, having trust and faith in his ability to provide with our understanding that we have work to do.

Consider that when spring comes, the farmer plants the seeds. God causes those seeds to grow, but the farmer needs to do the work God asks him to do. There is no harvest without an obedient farmer.

When we recognized that 2023 might be a hard year financially, we knew that to continue to tithe at the level we wanted, we might need to make sacrifices in other areas. But we also knew that continuing with our principles of stewardship and prosperity with a purpose had to remain consistent. It can be difficult to keep giving when finances feel uncertain, but we have faith in God's ability to provide when we remain obedient.

That's what provision is.

Uncommon financial freedom is designing your lifestyle within your means.

It will look different for everyone. You might not take fancy yacht trips or a cruise across the Pacific, but maybe you don't want to. Wherever you're at, using these guidelines to establish a positive path forward financially, you can design your own version of uncommon freedom. It's a complete lifestyle that encompasses not only your financial status but your marriage and family, too.

CHAPTER 5

BUILD A BULLETPROOF MARRIAGE

What does the average marriage look like?

On a continuum, a marriage ready for divorce is at the bottom of the scale at 0 percent. A marriage at 100 percent is uncommon. Most people are somewhere in the middle, a 50 percent average, with ideas and thoughts of divorce floating around though not yet having made landfall.

These are marriages that are stuck in the middle, doing little more than surviving.

An average marriage is a distracted marriage, one that's more complacent rather than on fire. It's two people swimming in their own streams. There's not much honesty or passion, which means there's very little unity.

At best, it's two people who are companions and not much more. Their needs aren't being met.

Average marriages, unless intentional work is put into them, only shift down the continuum toward 0 percent. When needs aren't met, we look elsewhere for them, whether in friendships, alcohol, pornography, shopping, or affairs—there's an endless supply of distractions for distracted marriages.

In the health world, we would say a person is in the non-sick stage. They haven't yet been diagnosed or medicated for an illness, but they are on the path toward it. Marriages that are stuck in the middle are on the road to a crisis. They're one empty nest away from getting divorced.

Whether we're talking about health or marriage, people slide to average (and eventually to the bottom) because it's easy to be passive and let life happen to us, allowing it to carry us downstream instead of setting goals and rowing upstream.

Average, stuck-in-the-middle couples take one trip a year, maybe, instead of consistent dates and getaways. They find comfort in routine instead of joy in pouring care and love into the other person. They have separate bank accounts and do other things that entertain the idea that a divorce could someday be an option. They disrespect each other in public.

They put their kids first, before the health of the marriage, because maybe it's easier to redirect attention and love to kids who would return it better than their spouse is able. It's easier to love a little daughter or son than a spouse who might let you down.

They confide in or form emotional connections with someone of the opposite sex, or in people who won't advocate for their marriage. Instead of stewarding their marriage relationship, giving the other person the benefit of the doubt and assuming that they have the best intentions in a situation, an average marriage trends downstream. Unforgiveness and an incredible memory for all the things the other person did wrong help feed that downstream current. There's a detailed score sheet of wrongs, and the idea grows that maybe a different life, one all on your own, would be better.

Moving toward the uncommon 100 percent means a different approach entirely. The score sheet is one of all the good a spouse has done. It's a marriage that has surrounded itself with people who will advocate for the marriage (as long as there is no abuse), respecting the couple's commitment to marriage. They have a healthy balance of time alone and time together.

THREE WAYS TO MAKE OR BREAK A MARRIAGE

Nearly every fight in a marriage shares the same roots.

Of all the arguments you could possibly have with your spouse, and all the reasons you think you're fighting, it usually boils down to one of two reasons. Fighting—no matter what it looks like or even what it's supposedly about—is simply about money and sex, in that order.[13]

13. Lisa Smith, "The No. 1 Reason Why Couples Fight," Investopedia, last modified November 28, 2021, https://www.investopedia.com/articles/pf/07/couples-finance.asp.

Two not-so-simple subjects, as it turns out.

Unfortunately, fights about these two things often share the same resolution tactic: poor communication. These two can make or break your marriage. So, let's talk about *how to talk about* money, sex, and marriage.

Let's start with money.

Money has the potential to bring joy and freedom to a marriage, but only if used right.

Poor finances, whether because of a lack of income or too much debt, grates on a marriage. Yet wealth can give you the comforts and distractions that actually cover up the things going wrong in your marriage. These substitutes might work for a while, but they're not enough to keep a marriage relationship together.

It's not just the stress of how much money, but who is controlling it.

Sharing finances, whether you're wealthy or not, is difficult. Early in our marriage, I worked hard at being a good steward, but I know it was a struggle for both of us. Bekah reminded me that at times, she felt strangled by the limitations I'd placed on how we would spend money, but we were able to work out a win-win solution.

In marriages where compromise isn't on the table (or where one or both of the people refuse to compromise or give an inch), a spouse will either spend the marriage into oblivion or hold onto finances so tightly that the other person feels like they can't spend money.

Both are extreme results of a lack of trust, and that's where you see the trouble start. When there is no compromise, the tension doesn't resolve. It finds a path of least resistance instead.

Like money, sex can be misused. Instead of an expression of love and intimate connection, it becomes about control.

A lack of sex, or selfish sex, creates untold problems in a marriage. When there is no interest in serving each other, intimacy disappears. This can happen without intending to; in busy lives, couples have to prioritize time for romantic dates and sex instead of assuming it'll "just happen."

Getting the money and sex right means both partners have to be good about communicating. An inability to communicate what each person needs means you end up in a lot of stupid fights.

Consider the story of a woman who'd had a busy day at home. She didn't feel like making dinner that night, and when her husband arrived, she asked him if he'd like to go out.

He'd had a busy day at work and really just wanted to stay home. So he told her no, he didn't want to go out.

The wife was hurt and spent most of the evening holding him at an emotional distance. She was upset until it occurred to her that what she should have said was what she really needed: *I'm not up for making dinner tonight. I don't care if you make dinner, if we go out, or if we order in, but I can't make the meal tonight.*

Too often, we assume our spouse knows what we need. We communicate based on that assumption and instead of being clear about what we need, we end up fighting about peripherals and racking up a scorecard against each other for all the slights and wrongs done to us.

I know this from experience.

In our first year of marriage, we didn't have a lot of money. Christmas rolled around, our first as an engaged couple, and we were all set to make some big memories celebrating with my family as Bekah was visiting me in Ohio from her home in Oregon. Her family Christmas traditions didn't include lots of Christmas gifts, though they did make sure that each person got one thing they really wanted, and that the special gift was always given last as kind of the big hurrah.

I didn't realize this. Bekah hadn't told me.

We exchanged a few small gifts until she got her last gift from me. It was a small box, nothing too big, but in her mind, this gift was going to be amazing. After all, this was the last present.

AN UNCOMMON
MARRIAGE IS MADE
OF TWO PEOPLE
WHO COMMUNICATE
WANTS, NEEDS,
PREFERENCES,
AND EXPECTATIONS
ABOUT EVERYTHING...

I watched as she opened the box. Her eyes were full of expectation as she reached in and pulled out . . . a plastic tennis ball holder that you clip to your shorts. I thought it was a great and practical gift because we played a lot of tennis and the shorts we wore didn't have pockets. But the look on her face told me otherwise.

I like to think I made it up to Bekah several years later when I got her a tennis bracelet and wrapped it up in that tennis ball holder container as a kind of joke. And oddly, we still have that plastic tennis ball holder today. Bekah likes to use it as a prop on stage during some of her talks.

But it's a memory that reminds us we can't assume the other spouse knows what we want. It's a great story to tell now but was horribly painful at the time. We never had a conversation about expectations, about how our families did holidays (and believe me, our families are drastically different).

Expectations and the assumptions they come with are potent relationship killers. We all come into a marriage with complicated histories and traditions, and the other spouse has no way of knowing them unless we communicate clearly. Bekah and I both learned that what we thought was "normal" was what we grew up with. We assumed that was normal for the other as well, but boy were we wrong!

An uncommon marriage is made of two people who communicate wants, needs, preferences, and expectations about everything, including money and sex, instead of assuming the other should have figured it out by now.

THERE WILL BE CONFLICT . . .
BUT IT DOESN'T HAVE TO DESTROY

With communication (and miscommunication) comes conflict.

When it comes to how Bekah and I handle conflict, we're both a little spicy.

At the beginning of our marriage, we weren't gentle in handling conflict. Bekah's family isn't prone to being loud and sometimes avoids conflict in favor of keeping the peace. But they always come together and work things out, never leaving something unfinished and festering.

My family is different. With four boys and a lot of sarcasm, we lacked sensitivity and were very intense. I didn't recognize that early on, which created some friction in our marriage.

As any newlywed knows, though, there's no shortage of advice on how to handle the inevitable conflict that will hit your marriage about five minutes after saying "I do."

Me and Bek on our wedding day.

"Don't go to bed angry," is the standard advice most of us hear, but as Bekah has pointed out to me, sometimes you just need to go to bed and start fresh the next morning. The sooner you talk about something, the better, obviously, because the more time that passes, the more clarity is lost. The fight becomes about all kinds of additional things that have built up in the long stretch of anger.

Our biggest fights have been those unresolved things that festered and then came back, those disagreements or disappointments that were never dealt with right away. That's why it's important to get the conversation as close to the conflict as possible, not leaving each other the space to fill in the blank for who's to blame.

A technique we use (even with our kids) is to ask what story you're telling yourself. It might look like this:

"Dad, he tried to knock me over!"

"Wait a minute. The fact is he bumped you."

"Yeah! He tried to knock me over!"

"No, that's the story you're telling yourself, that he intended to knock you over. But all you actually know is that he bumped you."

What is the fact and what is the story you're telling yourself?

When something happens and you're ready to fight, take a breath. Pause. Breathe. And then ask yourself: "What are the true facts and what is the story I'm telling myself?"

Going back to Ohio created friction early in our marriage. I had most of my family and two decades of friend connections there, while Bekah only had a few high school and college friends who were still in the area. Yet for some reason we assumed we should always go for the same amount of time. I had dozens of people to spend time with and Bekah had very few. This led to days of boredom for Bekah while I was spending time with my brothers (who were still teenagers and unmarried) and having a blast with high school and college friends. In addition, the drastically different dynamics of our two families of origin revealed themselves on these visits.

That, along with some other issues, led us to counseling with our pastor. As we were spilling our guts, he said something so simple it astounds me to this day that we didn't see it ourselves.

"Why do you both have to go to Ohio for the same amount of time?" he asked us during one session. "Kevin, why don't you go for a longer visit, and Bekah just for a few days?"

Boom. We'd made it so hard, and it took an outside perspective to bring clarity to the problem.

From then on, the visits back to Ohio went much better. Bekah's visit was better. My visit was better. Most of the stress we dealt with on these trips was gone.

Getting married young meant we didn't have sisters-in-law or brothers-in-law to look to for an example. All we knew was how our parents were, and we brought those struggles into the marriage. Because we didn't understand what was at work, we couldn't see each other's perspective and understand the differences of where we came from and how we learned marriage should be. Instead of partners, we were adversaries.

Today, we are speaking the same language.

Back then, we were fighting and unable to understand each other.

When you're at an impasse, counseling is a good idea. You need the outside perspective. Uncommon freedom in marriage means embracing quality mentorship and help.

I want to end with another terrible statement I've heard, and that's "if you're in a good marriage, you never really fight." It's possible two people have personalities that make that possible, but I doubt it. Bekah and I have always had disagreements, but they are few and far between at this point. We've had years of practice on how to resolve them, no matter how heated they might get. Conflict isn't necessarily unhealthy, as long as it is resolved. In a way, you learn about each other, about underlying assumptions, and about how to communicate with the other person.

Unhealthy conflict is something else.

It's constant, heated, goes unresolved, and picks up where you left off the next time something happens. It is exponential, adding more fuel to the fire and ultimately culminating in an unhappy married life that plods on in resentment or divorce.

ISOLATION IN MARRIAGE IS NOT A MARRIAGE

HALT.

Hungry. Angry. Lonely. Tired.

This is when a person breaks. It's when sex addicts turn to porn or food addicts eat everything in the cupboard. From my coaching experience, when a client isolates themselves, 90 percent of the time they are struggling and about to fall.

One of the most difficult times in our marriage happened early on. I was in the Marine Corps, attending Ground Supply Officer's School for a few months in Camp Lejeune, North Carolina while Bekah stayed in Quantico, Virginia to teach summer school. Our plan was for me to commute back to Virginia every few weeks while we were living in different places.

Bekah later told me that it was difficult for her to articulate the isolation and loneliness she felt at the time. I was gone most of the time, immersed in a world she didn't understand. Bekah was isolated. We didn't have a faith community that we were connected to. Her job was something she stepped into out of necessity, not really knowing anyone. And the women she managed to meet didn't have the same interests that she did. Most of her time was spent alone. Her life consisted of work, jogging alone on the beach, and sitting in our apartment by herself.

I didn't realize how dangerous this was to our marriage.

When one partner is isolated and alone, their cup is empty. Situations that should have been easier to handle instead echo with massive reverb in the emptiness; small things become big things quickly.

This was clear when, the first weekend I went home to see Bekah, I made the long drive with a female classmate. Her husband and kids also were still living in the Quantico area so instead of both driving our own cars, we saved money on gas and drove together. Nothing had happened, other than talking, but for Bekah it felt like I had crossed some boundaries spending that much time with another woman. This was the start of a difficult time. The enemy used this situation to plant seeds of doubt and distrust. It was like a wound that festered.

After Bekah finished teaching summer school in Virginia, she was finally able to join me in North Carolina. To her, North Carolina wasn't much different. It seemed as if I had a busy life on the base, spending time in the barracks, while she was left alone in a tiny apartment.

On top of that, my supply school classmates spent a lot of time together, and on weekends families were invited to join. The presence of the female officer that I had spent that car ride with continued to be a challenge for Bekah, and that wound continued to fester without us addressing it.

To get out of the apartment, Bekah spent time at the gym on the base. She told me that she started to imagine how she might be appreciated by the men there since I wasn't showing her any appreciation at home. She never acted on her desire for attention from others, though the thought of doing so was there. Bekah felt like I'd abandoned her. And in a way, I had. I was pursuing my dream, plugged into the military community, feeling a sense of purpose, and she was left alone.

On the night of our fourth anniversary, we had plans to go out, but I was late getting home. When I arrived, Bekah was sobbing and I was caught off guard.

"I might be done with this marriage," she said. She'd been carrying around a lot of pain and hurt, but we'd never resolved it. "I don't know how much longer I can live like this."

Shortly after this admission, we made our move to Okinawa, Japan for my assigned duty station and it looked like a chance for a fresh start. At first, Bekah still struggled with being alone until we got plugged into the community and we worked on resolving the issues that started back in supply school.

When we look back on our time in Japan, we have some of our best memories there. But it didn't start out that way. A change of scenery doesn't equal a change of heart and we won't forget the work it took to get past those dark times when our marriage almost ended just a few years after starting.

Our Okinawa community

Perhaps Bekah's internal warning system wasn't so off; that supply officer and her husband eventually got a divorce. And that could easily have been us.

Unhealed and unresolved hurt and anger fester until something breaks. Isolation and lack of community make you and your marriage grow apart.

GROWING TOGETHER INSTEAD OF APART

Uncommon freedom, when it comes to marriage, is when both people grow together.

If one person wants to grow—to change habits, to change what they put into their mind and body—and the other does not, how can the marriage navigate it? You might not always both be in the same boat, but you should at least be going in the same direction.

An uncommon marriage is one where both people share the same goals and dreams. Dreams for your kids, the activities you'd like to do, what your retirement will look like—it's future oriented and you're both on the same wavelength. You're going to the same place and you'll arrive at the same time.

There is a spiritual component to this. The Bible makes clear the importance God places on believers not "yoking" themselves to unbelief, whether it's in marriage or some other kind of partnership. Things that are unmatched and partnered together will cause destruction in the end (Matthew 9:16–17).

Bekah has lots of ideas. I have lots of ideas. We're not competing with each other. Why can't we come alongside and cheer for each other?

Early on, as Bekah started her health journey, I didn't have the desire to cheer her on. We weren't going in the same direction, and that made it more challenging for her. Now we are headed in the same direction, and it's a true partnership.

We still have our struggles. We partnered in our health journey together, but there are always new things that pop up in a marriage where both people have to agree to partner again.

Our daughter Evie is an example.

In August of 2017, our friends Chris and Jihae took Evie in as a foster child when she was about two weeks old. They already had four kids, their youngest having been adopted through the foster care system just a few months earlier. Bekah and I remembered what sleepless nights with a newborn were like, and we offered to take Evie for a night so Chris and Jihae could get some recuperative rest.

Jihae brought Evie over on Wednesday, September 20, 2017. I honestly had no special interest in Evie, other than helping out our friends by watching their newborn foster child. But shortly after Jihae left, it was time to feed Evie, so I got a bottle ready and went to pick her up. As I lifted Evie from her car seat and held her for the very first time, I clearly felt and heard God tell me, "Kevin, this is your daughter. Are you going to step up and be her dad?"

Um . . . what? It couldn't have been more clear if God had spoken out loud to me. Plus, I felt this warm rush of love that was already connecting me to Evie as her dad. But even though my heart was instantly filled with the love of a father for Evie I was still very confused. I hadn't been expecting that at all!

The next morning, to test the waters, I joked to Bekah, "Maybe we should adopt Evie?"

Her immediate reply was, "Absolutely not!"

I felt God was telling us we should adopt her, but Bekah wasn't sure. She hadn't heard the same message from God that I had. She told me she wrestled with God about it, and it was clear initially that this was not at all what she wanted to do. Our boys were past the diapers, bottles, and temper tantrums stage, and going back to that wasn't something she wanted to do.

In a sense, starting again with a new baby meant isolation and a loss of freedom for Bekah because our family life, and the new requirements that would come with it, would change. She was at a point in her life where she was coaching clients, speaking at events, traveling . . . . I hadn't been around for the daily care of the boys when they were young like Evie was and didn't fully realize what it involved.

But Bekah knew what a new infant would mean for her life.

No simple traveling. Late nights. Restricted schedules. Inconveniences we couldn't imagine. Raising a tiny human is a lot of work.

Plus, there would be a lot of emotional challenges dealing with adoption courts and birth parents. It wasn't going to be easy.

I felt like this was God's calling for us, but Bekah—as much as she loved Evie and wanted to be in her life—wasn't sure about making the leap to adoption and being her mom. She trusted what God was telling me was true, but she wasn't feeling that herself. She told me that at first, it felt as if I was choosing Evie over the family we'd been raising, discounting what they might feel about it.

We were at an impasse, with one spouse wanting to go one direction and the other a different direction.

Eventually, we both agreed to take the leap and adopted Evie.

There were some very difficult seasons, including a disconnect between Bekah and Evie early on, but in the end, we discovered that our family needed Evie as much as she needed us. Our boys needed her. I needed her. Bekah needed her.

God has used Evie to consistently change our priorities and how we go through our day. He has used her to bring attention to times we need to slow down, to put our focus back on Him and His time, to bring healing and realization in our lives through ways we'd not imagined.

In our small group and immediate community, we had support from several other families who had also been involved in foster care and adoption. Being part of a community that can relate is so important.

Stealing kisses from Evie in 2019.

But we also went to a counselor to help work through the whole process and transition. The truth is, like so many other areas of life, we are still contending. While struggles aren't constant, we have to contend daily because growth stops when we no longer contend.

The final chapter of Proverbs closes out all its wisdom by describing an incredible woman. I always think of Bekah as the Proverbs 31 woman. She's energetic and strong, a hard worker with an industrious spirit. She partners with me, works alongside me. She's told me that she admires that I have integrity, that I'm ambitious and never settle for "good enough." There are always goals and potential for growth on the horizon.

We are two individuals, yet we are true partners, mutually respecting and submitting to each other so we each shine in the areas we're good at. We're not in competition with each other, but instead, build each other up. Instead of butting heads to see who gets to be in control, we can be strong together without making someone less.

Author Gary Thomas describes it like a ballet in his book *Cherish*, borrowing from George Balanchine, the great ballet choreographer. Balanchine once said that "ballet is woman." What he meant was that the best male dancers recognize that people come to the ballet to see the graceful woman. The male dancer's job is to help her be more than she could be on her own by lifting her, supporting her, and catching her. He makes the beautiful even more beautiful. If a male dancer does his job and helps the female dancer do her job, at the end of the ballet there is thunderous applause.

A marriage can't be about the life, career, or joy of one over the other. We serve together. We see the best in each other. It's a beautiful dance.

Not every marriage has that. But it could.

For starters, understand that commitment must be all in. James 1:8 tells us that a double-minded man is unstable in everything he does, and that's especially true in a marriage. There can be no bridges left to give yourself an out. All of your energy is committed to the marriage. Too many people have settled for "we'll give it a try," meaning that they've left a door open to leave, in case trying doesn't work. Burning the bridges of other options is essential.

Next, change from being good at fault-finding to being grateful. Faults are easy to find, but finding good qualities you appreciate takes work. Can you find one thing every day that you appreciate about your spouse? That's not an easy step, but it is simple. Find something each day.

From there, begin to understand the value of fulfillment and purpose, two undervalued concepts that are the driver for so much that we do.

Men, do you know when your wife is in her element? When she's at her best, finding joy and fulfillment in what she's doing? How can you help her get there?

Women, do you know the same for your husband? Many men go to jobs they don't like, jobs that are unfulfilling. Would you give them permission and freedom to experiment or find a side gig that would bring them joy? Or do you pressure them to go the path you want them to go?

I know I've been blessed in this area.

Not everyone is going to be in business together like Bekah and me, but I've found that it has put our mission and intimacy in high gear. There are challenges, to be sure; sometimes *not* talking business is our goal. We have to plan our time for parenting, business, and personal time. That requires boundaries. But we left careers and jobs to find what gave us purpose and fulfillment, and our marriage is stronger because of it.

Whether you go into business together or not, it's important to know each other's strengths and weaknesses.

I'm good at numbers, and while we talk about finances together, I handle more of the budgeting and function as our company's CFO. Bekah has other skills that I leave to her. It's important to understand what lane we're in. In our work, we've figured out that Bekah is more creative while I'm better at editing. Instead of butting heads and fighting to both be creative, we've learned a kind of dance based on what we're best at.

And finally, prioritize *at least* a weekly date. We're big fans of quarterly retreats, too! Our retreats, especially the fourth quarter, have become the perfect setting for us to plan for our future together.[14] The change of scenery and limited distractions from day-to-day life really lend to a different environment of relaxation

---

14. Go to *BekandKev.com/Yearly-Reflection-Worksheet* for a great resource you can use during your fourth quarter retreat to reflect on the past year and plan your future goals for the new year!

and creativity. Though it's ideal to get away for these retreats, this is going to look different for everyone depending on what stage your family is in. Quarterly getaways may seem out of reach due to logistical or financial reasons for some, but I'd really like to challenge you to push through those barriers to have quality time with your spouse. To be clear, do not go into debt or create further hardship for your family to achieve this, but you may surprise yourself with how much you can do with a little creativity.

A bulletproof marriage doesn't happen to you; remember that the current always carries you downstream. Instead, it's something you fight for, including setting aside time to be with your spouse without the distraction of family and work and worry.

CHAPTER 6

PARENT WITH
A PURPOSE

Until the 1700s, society was mostly agrarian. Village and farm life was king. People spent their time in the home, making the goods they needed and the food they'd eat.

Each home was a place of self-sustaining life.

Then the Industrial Revolution happened. Science and technology blew open the doors of possibility and production, and people flocked to the cities. Factories sprang up faster than grain in the fields. The price of goods dropped and people could own things they'd never been able to afford back in the day. Entire economic systems changed, but so did family life.

What we think of as normal, that nine-to-five job where one (or both) parents head off to work to earn a living, was brought about by the Industrial Revolution, an advance that stole parents (and even children) away from the home. Thanks to the Industrial Revolution, the family became an economic unit, a consumer, and an easy target. It was splintered as the focus shifted outside of the home as the way to sustain life.

Unfortunately, society has continued on that trajectory.

As a family, we decided to purposefully push against that. One of the things we did was create a family crest that would serve as a reminder of what God had promised us. We chose Deuteronomy 28:1–14 as the scriptural guiding principle. We, as a family, would live our lives according to God's promise, and in turn, he would keep those promises. We re-read the passage often, and have put the family crest on display in our house as a reminder.

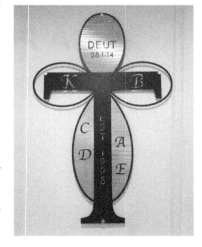

While I'd encourage you to sit down with your family and create your own family crest, at the very least, be purposeful in pushing back against the downstream flow that wants to destroy your family.

UNCOMMON PARENTING CREATES
AWESOME FUTURE ADULTS

In today's homes, most parents are either stuck and struggling or averaging somewhere in the middle. It's estimated that by the time your kids are twelve years old, you'll have spent 75 percent of the time and influence you'll ever have with them.

Parents who are stuck and struggling have neither quality nor quantity to give to their kids. Average parents think "quality" parenting can replace quantity, and rely on passive intuition or instinct as their guide. The uncommon parent is intentional and always learning, realizing that quality *and* quantity are necessary.

I'm going to go out on a limb and say that average parents won't create the adults we need for the future. Most of us have become aware of the statistics of young adults living at home,[15] struggling with mental health issues,[16] marrying later if at all—the list goes on. It would be easy to shake a fist at the younger generations and wonder why they can't get their act together like those generations before them.

The culprit, quite often, isn't "bad" parenting, but average parenting.

Hear me out on this.

First, realize that the average at any given moment takes into account all of society, adds it up, and finds the middle. That means as society shifts up or down, the average moves accordingly. So, when it comes to parenting today, where are we at with the average? What does today's average parent and home look like? And what will your uncommon parenting create?

---

15. Richard Fry, "It's Becoming More Common for Young Adults to Live at Home—and for Longer Stretches," Pew Research Center, May 5, 2017, https://www.pewresearch.org/fact-tank/2017/05/05/its-becoming-morecommon-for-young-adults-to-live-at-home-and-for-longer-stretches/.
16. "Generation Z and Mental Health," The Annie E. Casey Foundation, March 3, 2021, https://www.aecf.org/blog/generation-z-and-mental-health.

UNCOMMON PARENTS LET THEIR CHILDREN MAKE CHOICES

The average parent is child-centric.

That sounds like good "quality" parenting, but it's unhealthy. Making the child the center of the home (and the universe) feeds into narcissistic tendencies.

These are parents who constantly bail their kids out of trouble, defending them from all accusations and rarely letting them feel the consequences of their actions.

These are parents who travel all over the country, spending thousands of dollars they don't have on athletic tournaments for kids as young as elementary age. They put hardship on the family finances, split up the family to do the traveling, and give their children the false belief that they will likely make it as a professional athlete. Money that could go for a family vacation, a mission trip, or even a side business is tossed through the net or goalposts and gone forever.

Because there's such a focus on the child, there's not a lot of awareness of what kind of cultural influences are at work in their kids. Child-centric parents develop a lack of intentionality.

As an uncommon parent, your children will experience the outcome of their choices, whether good or bad. They'll have a realistic understanding of where they belong in the family home and finances.

UNCOMMON PARENTS ARE PRESENT

Our culture takes pride in being busy, and that goes for families. A busy family whose kids are in lots of activities gets accolades.

But busy parents let busyness drive them, instead of being intentional about how they parent. They've been fooled into thinking that proximity is the same as presence; that being co-located is the same as connecting.

That means fathers who are focused on providing instead of fathering. They watch from the sidelines, instead of being out there on the court with their kids in their lives. They work hard to earn money and be a good provider but miss the more important calling to be a father.

As an uncommon parent, you won't let busyness or activity get in front of meaningful relationships with your kids.

UNCOMMON PARENTS WANT STRONG KIDS

Having happy kids at any given moment isn't the goal.

Average parents who focus on having happy kids aren't looking at the future. They aren't thinking about raising successful, healthy adults capable of facing all the things that come with adulthood. Instead of making parenting decisions with future adulthood in mind, the average parent is more concerned that their kids are happy right now.

I get it.

Who wants to do battle daily, trying to instill self-control and teach proper behavior? It's easier to cave to whining and manipulative kids, giving them what they want instead of what they need because that makes them happy in the moment.

As an uncommon parent, you'll raise strong kids capable of dealing with adulthood instead of chasing after whatever makes them happy in the current moment.

UNCOMMON PARENTS LET THEIR KIDS
BE THEIR OWN PEOPLE

The average parent has a lot of identity attached to their kids.

Whether it's behavior, performance, throwing fancy parties, or all of the crazy social media standards that trend, parents are trying to live through their kids and in comparison to people around them.

I've seen parents live vicariously through their kids, whether it's in sports, grades, or other activities. They scream at the refs, and they build the science fair projects. These are parents who somehow feel validated personally if their child can achieve something in place of them.

Bekah has noticed that moms, in particular, quickly become trapped in making their whole identity revolve around their household success. That becomes their identity; they become a hashtag version of a parent, a #MommaBear who won't let anyone discipline their naughty child, or a #PerfectMom who tries to keep the home like a flawless Instagram feed. They wear themselves out and find ways to decompress that are less than healthy.

As an uncommon parent, you won't feel the need to live vicariously or find meaning in life through your children.

UNCOMMON PARENTS TAKE A ROLE AS TEACHER

In Jordan Peterson's book *12 Rules For Life*, rule five is to not let our children do anything that makes us not like them.

Who wants to live with someone they don't like? Why do we allow our children to become that person? I can guarantee you that if you don't like being around your kids, no one else does, either.

This means taking an active and purposeful role in training them so they will be able to navigate the world as an adult. It's easy to forget that behavior is learned, and simple things like sitting down to eat don't come naturally. As Peterson points out, children test the boundaries of behavior because that's how they find out what the limits are.

Yet average parents don't enforce the limits; in fact, too many assume someone else will.

The average parent has abdicated their role as the primary educator. They've allowed the school to set the standards in knowledge, discipline, culture, and emotional behavior. They've allowed the church to handle all of their kids' spiritual growth. They've allowed social media and peers to define what kind of behavior is acceptable.

As an uncommon parent, you understand the importance of teaching your kids how to behave, how to think, and how to live within boundaries. You won't pass off this most important role to anyone else.

PASSIVE PARENTING AND THE TRAP OF CONVENIENCE

If there's an underlying takeaway in all of what you just read, it's that parents can't be passive. They can't find the most convenient solution for right now and hope there's no downstream pull in the future.

Passive parenting means you are mostly concerned about convenience, allowing things to happen to your family and in your family without putting up a fight because you don't feel like fighting for that boundary today.

One rule we've tried to adopt is to never allow our kids to do something that we'll have to re-parent in the future. We don't always get it right, but we've learned it's better to train them properly the first time than to do it again when they're older. This doesn't mean setting impossible standards, but if you allow poor behavior when they're young, it's going to get so much worse when they're teenagers or even adults.

It's never been easier to parent for convenience than it is today with all the technology we have available.

Convenience says that a child who's quiet for hours while watching a screen makes it easier on the parent. While it's more convenient to let the electronics babysit our kids, it's not good for them in the long run. She's out of the way for a while, but when that screen is shut off, watch out. Our convenience now leads to serious problems and headaches later.

Henry Cloud echoes that same idea in his book *Boundaries for Leaders: Results, Relationships, and Being Ridiculously in Charge*, in which he says that "leaders get what they create, or what they allow". The same goes for parents. The behaviors will happen because our kids are human, but if we tolerate them, then our kids become intolerable.

It's not easy; trust me, I know. Our boys argue a lot. There's teenage moodiness creeping in. Their personalities are different. We don't have it perfectly figured out, but our goal isn't perfection. Our goal for their behavior is that our kids will be delightful around others, and that people won't groan when they see them coming. We want those hard, ugly moments to happen at home where we can deal with them and shape behaviors. If we wait until we're out in public and around people, it's too late and incredibly embarrassing. But we've also learned you can't control the future and embarrassment is just a part of parenting. Kids will become their own person as they get older. We can't live in fear that their personal decisions will embarrass us or ruin our reputation.

But there are some things in our power to affect. You know what I'm talking about.

You've seen parents with horribly behaved children carrying on in public or at events, the parents frantically trying to control behavior they've passively allowed at home as if it would magically work now when they need it. At home, it was about keeping the kids happy, placated, and not too much of a bother for busy parents. But what happens when you're not at home?

If you've never made your kids sit down and eat with the family and learn to carry on conversation at home, that behavior won't be available when you need it outside of the home.

If you've never been intentional in talking to your kids at home, when a crisis arises at school, that trust and connection isn't going to magically appear in the principal's office.

If you've never set rules about screen time and technology use at an early age, the fights you'll have about it when your kids are teenagers are going to be ones for the record books.

EVALUATING YOUR PARENTING STYLE

We all struggle, including Bekah and I, to hit the mark each day. In previous generations, parents weren't as hyper-aware of themselves as we are today.

It's not necessarily bad to consider how you're parenting and to pay attention to how other parents are doing things. Bekah and I were married nine years before we had kids, and we carefully observed parenting examples all around us. We decided what kind of parents we wanted to be like (and which ones we didn't). What books did these parents read? What did they do? What didn't they do? How did they handle themselves? What habits or patterns did they create in their home?

Careful observation is not the same as living comparatively. One is intentional, and one is at the mercy of the current situation. One helps prepare you while the other ends up trapping you in fear. Bekah has admitted to worrying about how to parent teenage boys and all the things that come with it, but we can't live in fear. We do what we can do, and we have to trust the rest to God.

It's also worth being aware of the things you bring into your family that come from your own parents. There are a lot of things I do that aren't necessarily beneficial, but they are things my parents did. Without being aware, I could easily continue the pattern of my parents and those before them instead of considering what I should do differently.

"I'm never going to be like my parents!" is the defiant cry of nearly every teenager. And yet, when our turn to be a parent comes around, in many ways we become Mini-Me versions of our parents.

The key is to continue the good things our parents did (and my parents and in-laws both did lots of good) and avoid making the same mistakes. We have to make a decision to change.

PUTTING INTENTIONALITY BACK IN PARENTING

Intentionality can seem like a buzzword; all it means is that what you do, you *intended* to do.

That means that circumstance didn't push you to a decision. Culture didn't push you to a decision. Weariness didn't push you to a decision. You thought about what to do, what that would cause, and made a choice.

Take mobile phones, for example. No parenting expert in the world advocates for children to have unfettered access to a phone. Our kids tell us they're the "only ones!" without a phone, but that's not true. There are a few others. It might not be "normal" to not have one, but normal is rarely excellent. And we want to raise excellent, Jesus-loving, generous adults.

I know some days are tough. Decision fatigue is a real thing.[17]

After a day full of battles and decisions, we use up most of our decision-making energy and tend to make bad decisions or choose the path of least resistance. So after work-home-church decision #7678, when your kid comes to you and whines and demands to watch more videos on the iPad, I get why it's easier to just say yes. A "no" comes loaded with more battles and decisions, and you're done for the day.

But being unintentional chooses the path of least resistance, and we can't do that as parents.

17. John Tierney, "Do You Suffer from Decision Fatigue?," The New York Times, August 17, 2011, https://www.nytimes.com/2011/08/21/magazine/do-you-suffer-fromdecision-fatigue.html.

BEING UNINTENTIONAL
CHOOSES THE PATH OF
LEAST RESISTANCE,
AND WE CAN'T DO
THAT AS PARENTS....
UNCOMMON PARENTING
IS INTENTIONAL.

If it means getting rid of things in your life that are sapping your energy and requiring too many decisions, then do it. Uncommon parenting is intentional.

Meal time is intentional. Family games or conversation time is intentional. TV time is intentional. Bedtime is intentional. Taking our kids on "dates" is intentional.

THE LAW OF FIRST MENTION

Having hard conversations is intentional, not waiting for a crisis to develop and force your hand. That means talking about their faith walk, friendships, associations, relationships . . . sex.

When studying scripture, there is something known as the law of first mention. The idea is that to understand a word or doctrine, we should find out where it is mentioned first. The doctrine might get fleshed out in more detail in the rest of scripture, but the first place we hear of something is the best place to start for understanding.

This applies to the hard conversations we should be having with our kids. We should be the source where they first hear about a lot of things, because having us as the original source of information and guidance adds its own meaning.

When we lived in Oregon, I signed up the family for a gym membership. While I worked out, the boys went to the gym's kids club. It was the time in the car, traveling to and from the gym, that was the great opportunity for connecting.

On one of the drives, we were listening to something on the radio that said babies were brought by storks. I knew they'd heard it, and I wanted to correct that idea before it settled in their minds.

"You understand that's not where babies come from, right?" I asked the boys. They were about ten, eight, and six years old.

"Where do they come from?" one asked.

While I certainly hadn't planned to go into the birds and the bees, that's what we did. I laid it all out, with the correct terms. At the end, with the car window down and armed with lots of new terminology, one of my boys started yelling "vagina!" out the window. While that wasn't awesome for me and the people on the sidewalk, it's important, as parents, to be the first ones to talk about these things. The law of first mention helps to put them in context and teach kids the truth.

In past generations, this would have been known as "the talk." Once and done.

But it should be seen as an *ongoing conversation* because as kids get older, they're going to have more questions. The world is certainly eager to be the first source to teach our kids about a lot of things, and it's only too happy to keep teaching them in an ongoing conversation. We have to do better than the world.

Sometimes, the conversations you have aren't the ones you think you should have. One of our boys loves to talk about cars. While Bekah would like to talk about deeper things, right now for my son, cars it is. Nothing gets him as animated as talking about cars, and so we talk about cars. That's sowing seeds into the relationship.

Other times, conversations are the ones you wish you didn't have. When it comes to the topic of sexual sin and porn, it's not a question of if our kids will come into contact with it, but when. Having an honest conversation where our kids feel safe means they know they can come to us and talk about it. We can tell them it's a sin, that we're not okay with it, and that it's worth waiting, even if everyone around us tells a different story.

BE INTENTIONAL ABOUT YOUR HOME CULTURE

Bekah has become more in tune with the Holy Spirit, becoming protective about what we allow in our home. One evening she realized that the audiobook CD our daughter had been listening to talked about demons. She didn't want her listening to that before she went to bed, no matter what kind of Christian perspective the story had.

Intentional parenting protects the presence that you allow into your home, whether it's in the entertainment you consume, the language you allow to be spoken, or the attitudes you allow to fester unresolved. Every decision we make creates the culture of our family life.

The way we set up chores, the way we discipline—everything we do as parents is in service to the kind of culture we want to intentionally create in our home, the kind of culture that we want those future adults to grow out of.

Culture starts immediately because the influence we have on our kids reduces as they get older. Aristotle said "give me a child until he is seven and I will show you the man," which means that

On DEBTs with our boys.

we have a limited window of influence. The first seven years of a child's life is when critical social and behavioral traits develop.[18]

We started taking our kids out on "dates" when they were young, investing time in them and making sure to provide opportunities for conversation. As they got older, they thought the idea of dates was gross because, well, teenagers.

We switched the name from "date" to DEBT: deep emotional bonding time. And as cool as those teens are, they still point out when they've missed their time with us, wondering when they get to go out. "Love" is spelled T-I-M-E.

Waiting to be intentional until it's more convenient, or you're less busy or less tired, or when your kids are more mature or pleasant to be around, will absolutely fail. Harry Chapin sang about this in the popular song "Cat's in the Cradle," where a father was too busy to be a father until the son was grown up; he unintentionally helped create a son who was too busy to spend time with him.

The irony is that those early years are usually the most challenging financially, so it's tempting to work more than you should. It's tempting to come home after a long day of work and zone out in the recliner in front of the TV.

Adjusting your standard of living is better than being absent because of work and weariness. I mean that. I'm very passionate about bringing more dads into the home to be actual fathers; kids learn a lot working side-by-side with their parents.

When I was a police officer, I had to really force myself to play board games, go to the park, or shoot hoops with my boys after a long shift. I was tired and wanted to zone out, but knew I didn't have that luxury if I wanted to connect with my boys. Bekah and

---

18. "Do the First 7 Years of Life Really Mean Everything?," Healthline, December 21, 2017, https://www.healthline.com/health/parenting/firstseven-years-of-childhood#By-the-age-of-7.

I have more freedom now, but if I had waited until today, my relationship with my boys wouldn't be the same.

WHAT ARE YOUR FAMILY VALUES?

We don't have a well-defined family mission statement, but we do have family values that we've listed throughout. Your family also has values. If you're intentional, you've decided what they'll be. If you're not intentional, you've let others determine them.

In the Tinter home, we believe:

- Persistence will grow us.
- Serving others is our calling.
- Our prosperity has a purpose.
- Our family sticks together.
- Fun and adventure is important.
- It's important to stick to our word.

These aren't just for Bekah and me but for the whole family. We find ways where we can all live these out.

For example, when Bekah and I give money, it doesn't cost the boys anything. We have to find ways that they can give and serve directly.

At a young age, we start teaching our kids how to do chores. We taught them to do their own laundry, for example, because when they are adults, they're going to need to know how to do that. We borrowed from Dave Ramsey and tied their commission (not allowance) to their chores: you don't do your chores, you don't get paid.

Evie helping with laundry.

This is how we teach them the value of money, that some goes to giving, some to saving, and some to spending. We want them to experience the joy of giving their *own* money, not just to the church, but also by letting them choose other ministries they want to help.

When it comes to our family values and sticky relationships, it's very important that our kids want to come back home someday.

No, we don't want them around all the time once they grow up, but we want to maintain a healthy and whole family connection. We can't wait until they're older; we have to start building that early on.

My brothers and I have a really good relationship. We love to spend time together, we have a lot of fun, and that's what I want for my kids. I don't want family rifts and rivalries and years of not speaking, so when we're working out an issue between our kids now, Bekah and I remind them that this is family and that while they might be at each other's throats now, someday they are going to be good friends.

One of the ways we deal with issues is to ask whether or not a decision is more likely to cause a problem or solve a problem. It's a reframing of the golden rule, basically.

"Was that more likely to cause a problem or solve a problem?" I might say to one of my kids after they hit the other, trying to get them to confront the situation honestly.

Parents can ask themselves this question, too.

Are the values you've created in your home—intentionally or not—going to create problems or solve problems?

CHASING THE GOAL, WITH A DETOUR THROUGH KENYA

We're working hard each day to instill the seven disciplines of uncommon freedom in our kids. Seeing far down that road as parents is tough because it's a very long road; what seems small today becomes exponential by the end. Every phase of raising kids is its own challenge.

We had three boys in four years; that's a lot of toddlers all at once. And while that's physically exhausting—ask Bekah about one toddler changing the other's diaper, and how much poop that means on the furniture—the heart worries are less. That perfect little toddler surely will grow up to be wonderful.

The elementary years are a sweet time. The kids love you for the most part, and your emotions aren't as high and low. You start to let them experience consequences for what they do, in a limited way. But it's a season that goes by in the blink of an eye.

And then you get to the pre-teen and teenage years.

You have to start letting go then (some days you'd really, really like to let them go, believe me). You've poured in and cared for them, but now you have to start stepping back. You have to allow them to experience the much bigger consequences of their decisions. There's more correction because teenagers are making stupid decisions, yet we still have to let them know we love them and that they're cherished. This is a time when disengaged parents have no trouble letting their kids go because they've been doing it all along. But some parents struggle and never let their kids go, creating adult babies.

We're all going to have regrets about parenting because not one of us is perfect. Some days we drop the ball, and there's room for grace when that happens. Like you, we're chasing that goal; paddling upstream isn't an arrival, but rather a continued effort.

In 2020, we took our boys to Kenya so they could experience serving others firsthand.

Talk about a culture shock for them (and us).

But we also saw our boys become engaged and considerate, willing to try whatever food was put in front of them, caring about the kids, and embracing the kindness the Kenyans showed them. We saw the best version of them where, stripped of technology and the comforts of home, they were still really good humans. At home, they might complain about going to school or wanting new shoes every few months, but we got to see what was deep inside them, free from all those distractions, there in Kenya.

We got to see their faces when they were presented with situations that would make even adults uncomfortable. And toward the end of the trip, we watched their expressions when we took them on a safari. Their faces lit up as they watched the animals through the window of the vehicle, chasing alongside the creatures that herded across the grassy lands.

On safari in Africa.

Elephants. Giraffes. Zebras. Wildebeest.

Lions.

The lions were incredible. Strong cats, full of purpose, fearless, living in a close-knit community.

Bekah and I are not at a point where we are uncommonly free as parents, but we're chasing it. We're running toward that goal.

As parents, we are not islands. We decide what group we will be a part of; we decide who and what we will model for the next generation. When I think of my kids, and what Bekah and I want to see for their future, I am reminded that it is important to make sure that we run with lions.

CHAPTER 7

RUN WITH LIONS

YOU CAN RUN WITH
LIONS, OR YOU
CAN RUN WITH
THE PREY. BOTH
OPPORTUNITIES
ARE PRESENT,
RIGHT NOW. WHO
YOU SURROUND
YOURSELF WITH IS
UP TO YOU.

You already know all the people you'll ever need to know.

The theory of "six degrees of separation," the idea that all people were connected socially by six or fewer people, has been around since 1929 but was popularized by Stanley Milgram in the 1960s.[19] Milgram used postal letters to test how many people it took to get from one person to a stranger using only personal friends as a connection; it averaged to be six people. In 2001, Duncan Watts, a sociologist from Columbia University, ran a similar experiment using email. He also discovered that the average number of people it took to connect everyone was six.

In your sphere of influence, the right people are already there, somehow connected to you. Most of us don't really tap into it, but the reality is that opportunity is already in your orbit.

Do you believe it?

You can run with lions, or you can run with the prey. Both opportunities are present, right now. Who you surround yourself with is up to you.

ARE YOU IN THE WRONG COMMUNITY?

The worst community is no community.

The first negative thing God mentions in the Bible is that it isn't good for us to be alone (Genesis 2:18). We were made to be in a community.

Over the years, I've learned that clients who are unsuccessful isolate themselves from others. When they don't answer the phone when I call, 90 percent of the time it's because they are struggling.

---

19. Gardiner Morse, "The Science Behind Six Degrees," Harvard Business Review, February 2003. https://hbr.org/2003/02/the-science-behind-six-degrees.

Isolation is a check engine light. It's toxic. It convinces you you're a victim. Isolation is about us seeking our own desire, rejecting the wisdom and input from those around us (Proverbs 18:1).

Better than being alone is to have some community. Most people settle for average.

Average community is default community. It's unintentional. It's your high school friends, your neighbors, your family, and your coworkers—people who ended up in your life.

My experience with unintentional community conversation is a focus on people and what they've done, rather than on ideas or creating. It's gossip, favorite TV shows, and fluff, sitting around, eating, drinking, and watching screens.

Average community is about proximity instead of priority. Priority means to seek out people with the *intention* of building an uncommon community.

"Now hold on, Kevin, but I can't just shun my brother-in-law . . . ."

I'm not advocating excommunicating your family, but just because someone is in your family doesn't mean you have to spend a lot of time with them. God is pretty clear that who we are around is who we become (Psalm 1, Proverbs 12:26, 1 Corinthians 15:33).

Uncommon community is completely different from average community.

Instead of being a consumer and spectator, you're creating, thinking, and solving. You're talking about ideas, not people. You don't have to lower your standards and conversation to be in their company. In fact, if you're in uncommon community, you'll be challenged to raise your standards.

Uncommon community is filled with people who are abundant-minded and take extreme ownership of their lives. They aren't victims, complaining all the time, but are focused on creating opportunities for growth.

Our Arizona Freedom Crew hosted Kari Lake for a meet and greet in 2021.
Partner with like-minded people!

I mentioned earlier the well-known idea from Jim Rohn who said that we're "the average of the five people you spend the most time with." It's such a powerful idea. If you show me the five closest associations and friends that you have, I can show you your future self physically, financially, spiritually, and relationally.

Darren Hardy illustrates this idea well in a 2022 video. He starts by telling the story of "The Fox and the Grapes" from *Aesop's Fables*. A hungry fox is walking through the forest and sees a bunch of delicious grapes hanging from a branch. The fox crouches back and leaps, missing the grapes. After several more failed attempts, the fox starts to walk away, turning up his nose and saying "Those grapes were probably sour anyway." Aesop's moral was that it's easy to despise things in life that we can't (or lack the discipline to) reach.

Hardy takes it further, pointing out that people often give up too quickly after repeated attempts and failures, coming up with an excuse and letting bitterness take root. As Socrates said, "From the deepest desires often come the deadliest hate."

That hate moves outward toward others and turns into envy. Envy of a healthy body, envy of financial freedom, envy of business success. Hardy points out that Spanish novelist Carlos

Ruiz Zafon pegged that envy for what it really was: a religion of the mediocre. It comforts and soothes a person as it rots their soul. It justifies meanness and greed in a way that seems like they're virtuous qualities. Are you surrounding yourself with people who are practicing the religion of the mediocre?

Average community is passive, while uncommon community is very much an upstream activity.

PURSUING UNCOMMON COMMUNITY

Your network is your net worth, goes the saying.

There's truth in that, but I want to value relationships not because someone might be useful someday, but because of their capability to inspire greater things. To help put community into perspective, think of it as being made up of different spheres of connection and influence. It looks like three concentric circles:

- There's the core group, those who we're very close to, filled with people whose habits we want to develop.
- Next, there is a secondary, larger group who still have influence and are part of our network, but aren't part of our daily or immediate life.
- Finally, there is the peripheral group, which might include friends and family we don't want impacting our lives too closely but who are still present in our lives in some way.

If you want uncommon freedom in your life, your core group must have that same standard.

I have a regular poker game that I host. It's a large group, and not everyone there has bought into uncommon freedom. So I can tell you that my closest circle of community is in the poker group,

We thrive on community!

Our Raising Awesome Adults small group played a huge role in us adopting Evie.

My brothers, cousins and Aunt Kim & Uncle Paul make up the Birdie Bogie BBQ clan.

Our coaching community: it's a treat to do business with people you like!

My monthly poker group.

Our dinner party group of friends from Oregon.

My AZ Eagle's group.

but the entire poker group is not my closest circle. It's a question of whose influence I allow in my life.

Bekah and I have this crazy idea that if you want something, build it. Too many of us wait for someone to sit around and invite us to sit at their table. Why not build your own table? That means in every church Bekah and I have been to, we've become friends with the pastors and people on staff. We want to connect with people who have the ability to solve problems or take action. Being intentional about our sphere of influence has paid off. Sometimes, in all that upstream paddling, you meet connectors.

Connectors are people who serve others by connecting you to someone else who can change your whole life's trajectory. Of course, if you won't capitalize on the opportunity a connection provides, nothing comes from it; connection has to be paired with creativity and action. Connectors and builders are drawn to each other because they are all about building community.

RIGHT HABITS, WRONG PATH

When Bekah connected with Doug and Thea Wood, we didn't know how our lives would change.

We already had a lot of habits that made us successful, but our ladder was leaning up against the wrong building. I had more of a poverty mindset instead of an abundance mindset. When we would go to conferences, for example, I'd choose an off-site hotel to save money and end up missing out on building community and making important connections.

So even with our good habits, we were off course and on the wrong path.

We needed the right connection to help us see that, which happened to be the Woods. That right connection put us light-years ahead of where we would have been if we'd have had to figure it out ourselves. The Bible tells us that iron sharpens iron (Proverbs 21:17). The most dangerous thing is a dull blade, so get with people who keep you sharp.

John Maxwell is someone I've looked up to since 2012. I've read his books, listened to him on podcasts, and heard him speak live at several conferences. The Woods suggested the idea of having him speak at our Level Up conference in 2023 and when we reached out, he agreed. That meant we were able to meet him personally and have dinner with him, giving me a chance to find out what a genuine person John is. A few months later, I received a text inviting me to join John, Doug, and a few others at a golf course in Georgia.

I found myself spending time with these incredible leaders, surrounded by their knowledge and expertise, but even better, we had a chance to connect with someone at the resort who came to know the Lord that day. None of this would have happened, despite all of the positive habits we were making, if we'd stayed on that wrong path.

John Maxwell giving me advice on the golf course in May, 2023.

ESTABLISH BOUNDARIES BY MAKING DECISIONS EARLY ON

Daniel was wise to decide to pray and serve the true God long before it became illegal (Daniel 6).

He'd decided ahead of time, built the habit, and had the discipline in place. Despite being faced with a likely death sentence, he continued his daily prayer regimen. Prayer and being faithful to God was Daniel's priority. He'd designed his life around that.

When you plan and design your life, tough decisions aren't as difficult because you decide ahead of time. But you need to know what things are important to you.

As a family, we take at least three trips a year. Some of these trips are exotic vacations, others are simple visits to family or friends, and some are mission trips. They don't happen on their own if we don't plan for them. If you don't plan how you'll use your time, someone else will. The more successful you get, the more people want a piece of your time and if you don't know what your priorities are before that happens, you'll decide the wrong way, repeatedly, and it will become a habit.

It's not easy.

The fear of missing out can drive us to say yes to things we shouldn't, worried that if we say no we'll be excluded later. We think we'll no longer be relevant. But I've learned that if you have your priorities set, you grow your personal life and business. If those things are growing, you'll always be relevant.

Establishing boundaries means you decide for yourself, instead of letting people, fear, or circumstances make the call. Bad habits come from ceding that decision to things out of your control.

When you establish those boundaries and stick to your priorities, over time, the community you surround yourself with will change and begin to align with you. Your boundaries will naturally exclude some people or behaviors.

Even within a community, though, boundaries are necessary. The closer you get to people, the more your boundaries are muddied. The smaller and tighter a circle, the less distinct the boundaries become.

Some people are so disciplined about their boundaries that they come off as cold and indifferent to what people need from them. But consider all of the things that are vying for your attention, trying to pull you away from what you have decided are the most important things in your life. Things like faith, family, and health are easily forgotten if you don't have firm boundaries.

I'm giving you permission, right now, to create boundaries.

You don't have to let people tell you what to do when it collides with the life you've designed.

UNCOMMON COMMUNITY OPENS DOORS

Lurking in the back of my head was a dream of the Southwest.

A childhood family trip to the Grand Canyon and Lake Powell had planted the seed, and that sunny dream stuck with me.

Business trips to Tucson, Arizona, when it was raining back in Oregon, only added to the dream.

January 2016 was the breaking point. Walking the kids to school in pouring rain, with the memory of growing up in Cleveland with snow and rain, brought me to the end.

I'm so sick of this rain! I thought. And then: *We could move.*

Back home, dripping wet in the doorway, I asked Bekah what she thought about moving. She was open to the idea, so we started looking. We created a list of things we wanted, being intentional down to the last detail.

I wanted to move somewhere sunny. We were willing to visit snow, but not have it visit us. We traveled a lot, so we wanted to be near an airport with non-stop flights. That was a quality of life factor. We didn't want to be near Las Vegas. We wanted a culture that fit us.

But there was one problem: I wanted to get my pilot's license.

One of the reasons we'd stayed in Oregon so long was a particular flying school there would allow me to use the GI Bill to cover costs. We'd decided we'd stay there until I got my pilot's license, even though I wasn't actively pursuing it at that moment. There we were, drowning in Oregon's downpours because someday I was going to learn to fly.

All it took was a phone call with a friend.

He'd gotten his pilot's license and reminded me that there are *other* places to learn to fly, with or without the GI Bill's help.

Such a simple statement, but it blew my mind. Why hadn't that occurred to me? Obviously we knew that, but we'd gotten stuck. We'd designed a lifestyle, built a business, built good habits, and had even listed the ideal place to live. But without that pivotal conversation with my friend about getting my pilot's license elsewhere, we'd probably still be snorkeling down Oregon's roads.

An uncommon community doesn't feed victimhood; it helps you get unstuck.

Arizona, we love you.

5 WAYS TO DESTROY GREAT COMMUNITY

Remember those concentric circles, those different spheres of influence around you?

They seem like three strong walls surrounding you, an impenetrable stronghold. Unfortunately, the strong community we've created isn't usually destroyed from without, but from within.

#1: GOSSIP

God hates gossip (Proverbs 6:19), and that should be enough said. But gossip has the uncanny ability to start out as something else, sneaking in almost unrecognizable until the damage is done.

Prayer requests. Networking. Sharing. Discussing. A conversation that starts on one topic ends up being about a person you know. Awkward.

Knowing that I have to account for every careless word I've ever said (Matthew 12:36) has had an effect on me personally when it comes to controlling the tongue, but I've also been impacted by seeing how gossip destroys families, friendships, churches, and business relationships. There's no room for gossip in great community.

#2: LACK OF GRIT

Community is only as strong as the people in it.

People have a natural amount of grit, but we have to take responsibility to build on it. Since community becomes a self-fulfilling prophecy—you become what you're around—the people you allow to influence you will determine whether or not you'll develop grit, and whether your grit will influence someone else to do the same.

Microdosing adversity is a great way to build grit. That means getting used to conquering small challenges each day so the big ones that come along don't take you down. Walk up the stairs and skip the elevator. Read the book instead of a Wikipedia summary. Practice self-denial and delay of gratification. Stick to your health plan and to your budget.

If people are unwilling to tough out adversity as individuals, the entire community feels the weakening effects of it.

#3: DISCONNECTION

Distance can change or end communities, even if we don't intend for it to happen.

Bekah and I have moved around a lot, and I know this firsthand. People who were our best friends in one place shifted from our core sphere to the secondary sphere simply because of physical distance. Even changing churches in the same city has an impact.

While the connection is still there, it's changed and the influence is less direct.

Disconnection can be a driving force, though. After we'd made one of our moves, I realized I was seriously missing the group I'd been a part of back in the church where we used to live. I went to our new pastor and set about trying to rebuild a group because the disconnection was tangible.

Unfortunately, I ran into the problem of lacking common ground.

#4: LACK OF COMMON GROUND

A famous athlete who wasn't a believer was attending the church, and the pastor seemed enamored by the famous name. He wanted him to be a part of the group, but it made no sense in terms of the purpose of the group, particularly the potential influence that would be present from a non-believer.

That, along with some other decisions that were made in the church, made me realize it was time to walk away; having someone who wasn't a Christian in the group was a red flag. They might be the most amazing leader ever, a great entrepreneur even, but I didn't want someone speaking into my life who wasn't a follower of Christ.

John Maxwell talks about accepting the life you've been given instead of creating the life you want, and that same idea applies here. We want community by design, not default. Create the community you want instead of accepting what you're given.

Dinner with John Maxwell at our Level Up event in March, 2023.

In today's culture, citing a lack of common ground as a problem for building a community sounds backward. We need to carefully consider who we are allowing to speak into our lives. I don't care what skin color someone has, what side of the tracks they were born on, or what country they come from; if they are followers of Christ and have an ideology that fits with the boundaries and lifestyle I've designed for my faith, my family, and myself, I want to connect. As an example, Erika Acuna and her husband "Poncho" are some of our dearest friends. Erika came to this country illegally but has a burning desire to create her American Dream. I'd rather spend time with these hard-working people than a lazy natural-born American any day of the week! Erika recently earned her American citizenship and has more appreciation for this country than most Americans I know.

That doesn't mean people with a common connection always agree with each other. We all have different opinions or perspectives, and from godly people, that input is valuable. But diversity in opinion or understanding should come from people who share your priorities. History is filled with vast empires that collapsed under the weight of trying to unite too many disparate people groups who could not find commonality in culture and ideology.

Years ago, while attending a large men's Bible study group, a man sat next to me who was from a different ethnic group. I struck up a conversation in a way that people often do.

"Where are you from?" I asked.

"I'm from Cleveland."

"Hey, I'm from Cleveland, too!"

We soon found out we had some common interests (especially sports teams!), built on it, and to this day, we're still friends.

Community is held together by commonality. We connect with what we have in common, and then from there, can learn from what we don't. We are either walking together in the same direction, though we may talk about different things along the way, or we are walking apart in different directions and having to holler to be heard by others. The former is great community, while the latter is destructive.

Community starts by finding others who share our core principles and boundaries, and it crumbles when that common ground is gone.

#5: MISSION DRIFT

Sharing common ground means being in the same boat. But is everyone paddling in the same direction? What makes a core group of people so tight is that they are on the same mission.

People who aren't on the same mission aren't headed in the same direction.

We all know that people change. Personal goals and missions change as our lives change. That's not necessarily bad, but it means that the community can be damaged if that goes unrecognized. Close friends can still be friends, even if they shift away from the core group.

Think of a recovering drug addict. His life mission has seriously changed, and he can't go back to the same group of people if he wants to stay off drugs.

Uncommon community stays on mission.

GREAT COMMUNITY REQUIRES GREAT LEADERS

If you think you're a leader, but no one is following you, you're just out for a walk.

Leaders are community builders. They have a duplication effect on those following them, meaning that the habits and principles of the leader, whether overt or observed, show up in their followers.

You can tell a lot about a community by its leadership, and vice versa.

GREAT LEADERS LEAD LIKE LIONS

Alexander the Great said that he was "not afraid of an army of lions led by a sheep; I am afraid of an army of sheep led by a lion."

Even at the height of his power and success, Alexander would go to the front of the battle line and draw his sword to lead his men into battle. As a leader, he wasn't going to ask his men to do what he wasn't willing to do. Imagine what that was like, all hyped up on adrenaline, seeing your leader charging forward with you instead of sitting at a safe distance.

We follow as we are led.

What our leader models for us, we learn to do, even if it is beyond what we consider our limitations. Sheep led by a lion act like a lion. Lions led by a sheep act like a sheep.

The power of the leader to affect the followers is so profound because it's where duplication happens.

GREAT LEADERS DON'T OBSESS ABOUT NUMBERS

Our culture loves data. We love to brag about the number of followers, likes, wins, dollars, sales, and any other impressive number.

Jesus had thousands of people following him wherever he went, but it was his core group of just twelve disciples that he poured into and entrusted to spread the Gospel. Like the world, we Christians can get focused on the number of converts, but Jesus didn't tell us to go out and make converts. He said we should make disciples.

A small, close group of people has a greater impact than a stadium of converts.

That doesn't mean that numbers don't matter. When it comes to forming a core community, there's the struggle between too big and too little. Too few people become an echo chamber, but too many make it difficult for people to share.

Just don't let the numbers drive your action as a leader. Chasing numbers is wasted energy.

GREAT LEADERS KNOW WHEN TO LEAVE THE ROOM

John Maxwell has said that if you think you're the smartest guy in the room, it's time to find a different room. It's not a statement about some jerk who thinks he's a genius, but about realizing when it's time to move on from a community.

What's the group for? Why are you participating in it? Has it changed? Do you need to start a new group? Paddling upstream means you constantly review what's going on in the core group you're in.

The world has lots of eager followers who happily show up when something is created, but far too few great leaders. We're in desperate need of great leaders to duplicate, and that sometimes means moving on to a new group of people where that's possible.

GREAT LEADERS INSPIRE UNCOMMON FREEDOM

Commander's intent, which I introduced earlier in the book, is what the end of a successful operation should look like, concisely described by the leader of that mission. Everyone under the commander should be able to understand and unify around that end goal.

The key is to understand that the commander's intent doesn't describe *how* an operation will function, but *what the end goal is*. If things start to fall apart during the operation, that end goal never changes and the soldiers are still able to get there. They are free to think on their feet.

This might get me into a lot of trouble, but while Steve Jobs was a great, and eccentric, businessman who made popular products (yes, I do own an iPhone, iPad, and Apple computer), I don't think of him as a leader. He controlled everything down to the last detail, insisting that things were done his way. That is not the commander's intent.

Leaders have people that follow, not people that do what they're told. A leader inspires people to grow and eventually become leaders themselves; that's a maximized duplication effect that's about results, not nitpicking methods or absolute control.

GREAT LEADERS HAVE HIGHER LEVERAGE

When a pastor or prominent leader makes a change for the better, like getting healthy, people notice. When great leaders make big changes, it has high leverage. Great leaders use high leverage to move people.

Any time you make changes to your daily life, you're doing something differently from people around you and it stands out. The more you do something, the more personal momentum you gather to row upstream. You also start to rewire your brain.

James Clear, author of *Atomic Habits*, says that every decision you make casts a vote for the type of person you want to become. What's something you can do every day?

Let's say your marriage is struggling, so you decide to take one marriage retreat a year. Great. But it takes another full year to come around so you can cast that vote again. There needs to be something else that you can vote on more regularly to change the habits that are creating the problems.

Our identity often drives our habits and behaviors, and it is tough to "vote" outside of our identity.

Remember WWJD? We acted out of the identity of Jesus, modeling behavior after him. Who are you modeling your life after? What people have you let influence your thoughts and habits? What identity did you decide on? And even more frightening, who is modeling their life after you?

Before we moved to Arizona, I was blessed to have a pastor named Jared Roth who taught me a lot about lifestyle design, or how to be more intentional about designing your life. Most pastors tend to live under the tyranny of the urgent, so the fact that he was pursuing this path captured my attention. It had higher leverage.

He was entrepreneurial, doing a lot of business coaching as well as buying and rehabilitating struggling businesses. I joined a small group of guys he'd meet

Me with my pastor/mentor Jared Roth on our last Sunday in Oregon before moving to Arizona in 2016.

with each week, and he mentored us by teaching us the things he applied to life. I admired how he lived and what he accomplished, and I found an identity in that small group of men. I started to model my life after what he taught me. To this day I still keep him in my short list of people who have had some of the greatest impact on me.

There's also the old adage that if you want to go fast, you go alone, but if you want to go far, you go together. Without the influence of that pastor, I would not have been able to go as far as I have today.

CHAPTER 8

HONOR THE KING

The Irish elk is officially extinct.

Thousands of years ago, it roamed Ireland and parts of northern Europe, an animal so huge that it could get up to ten feet tall. A six-foot man might come up to the elk's jaw. Then add a rack of antlers on top of that—which could be up to 12 feet in length and five feet tall—and you had an animal with antlers as big as Goliath. Those antlers were a kind of crown of glory.

The Irish elk was a monster.

There are still elk today, but they are not the same.

Today's elk seem powerful, with their own amazing antlers that are coveted and collected. Despite how majestic they are to us, though, at most they might only get up to eight feet tall, antlers included. Next to an Irish elk, they seem small and weak.

In the book of Acts, we see a Christianity that is like the Irish elk.[20] It was powerful, and it moved massively. Believers were filled with a spiritual power that seemed fearless. Today's Christian tends to be a lesser version, one we've normalized. We think that the powerful move of God was for then, not for now. The smaller version seems to serve a good enough purpose. It has some power. It has "antlers." There are similarities, which fool us into thinking a facsimile is good enough.

Sightings of the Irish elk are still reported, and some say it is still around. Is it really extinct? Is it really gone? Who knows. But I do know that true Christianity isn't extinct.

Now and then, we glimpse it at work. Its glory, a reflection of the King, makes people stop and take notice. It stands out from average Christianity.

20. Eric Ludy, "Rack of Glory (Return of Majesty Trilogy)," YouTube video, 6:30, December 13, 2016, https://www.youtube.com/watch?v=bZiBnegXqIg.

AVERAGE CHRISTIANITY LIMPS ALONG

Average Christianity is everywhere.

It's not a threat to anyone, to any worldly plans or nefarious schemes. It has some effect, but doesn't exhibit the power it ought to, and for good reason. Average faith is easily seen in its disconnection from Christ and community. It makes the least amount of effort to bridge the gaps and ends up creating a Body of Christ that is discombobulated and ineffectual.

Consider what the average "Christian" looks like: occasionally attends church, but defaults to online church more often than not (especially post-pandemic).[21] Not in a small group. No time dedicated to prayer time and reading God's Word. Not being intentional about tithing, instead tossing whatever pocket change you have in the offering plate.

At its best, the average Christian is someone who checks the box once a week on Sunday morning and that's it, doing the bare minimum effort even though a vibrant faith would inspire so much more. Average Christianity embraces cheap grace, where we don't value what Jesus did for us, having more of a "fire insurance" mentality where the walk with Christ is more about staying out of hell than repentance.

When we get to Heaven, I have no doubt we will be surprised by who is and isn't there. This is where stuck Christians come in.

If you're saved and really believe the Gospel in your heart, you follow Jesus. We follow as we are led, so if we're raising hell, who are we following? Truly following Jesus brings about change, repentance, and transformation. It gets into every nook and

---

21. Not to ruffle feathers, but online church is not community, unless you're traveling and have no other option.

cranny of your life, and even the average Christian exhibits it to a slight degree.

The stuck Christian, however, shows very little of that repentance and victorious transformation because of either pride or shame. They think they don't need Jesus and live life as if the world comes first, or they think they don't deserve Jesus and live life in a perpetual state of shame. Either way, they both lack the freedom that comes from the presence of the Holy Spirit. The stuck Christian walks in pride or shame, with a tinge of bitterness toward God, instead of walking in faith and obedience and thriving in grace. They are completely floating downstream, no effort, no anchor.

When it comes to your faith, uncommon freedom starts when you understand grace completely, and you realize that there is a walking path stretching ahead of you that leaves room for continued growth instead of arrival.

Stuck Christians are small deer, most often looking at the headlights of the world barreling down on them. Average Christians are an elk, pushing forward as best they can. But when it comes to uncommon freedom and your faith, it's Irish elk all the way.

Standing out. Shockingly powerful. Bursting with the presence of the Holy Spirit.

POWER IN SPIRIT AND IN GRACE

I'll admit to struggling to reach (or even define) uncommon freedom in my own faith life.

Just like anyone else, it's a daily battle, and this was the hardest chapter in the book for me to write because God is so big and I still struggle to row upstream when it comes to my faith. Having confidence in the things I can't see takes courage, and I have to remind myself that courage isn't a final destination but a daily process I have to exercise. Faith is the area that almost all of us need the most growth in, myself included.

As I read the book of Daniel, I realized that one of the reasons he was such a threat to the Babylonians was that the Holy Spirit was empowering him to be fearless and upright. Yet I was still missing something.

It didn't completely click until I began reading a book about the Holy Spirit.[22] I realized I'd made the mistake of thinking that the Holy Spirit is an "it" instead of a person, and I didn't understand grace.

It's easy to understand having a relationship with Jesus, yet he said he was leaving us someone better, the Holy Spirit, and we need to embrace that if we are going to have Irish elk Christianity.

But we also need a better understanding of what grace is.

It's easy to see grace as receiving salvation we didn't deserve, but more difficult to also see grace as God's empowerment.

There are three times in my life where I've seen that empowerment visibly at work, where God has stepped in and made his presence significantly known.

The first big God moment came when I didn't get a job.

There was a law enforcement job I wanted because on paper it looked like everything was lining up and it was God's will. It would've been a miracle, and it seemed like it was going to happen. I was so sure it was mine, right up to the day another guy got it.

God is in control, was what Bekah and I told ourselves, but at the time, it hurt. It was confusing. That job was how we were going to create more margin and make our lives better.

---

22. John Bevere, *The Holy Spirit: An Introduction* (Lake Mary, FL: Messenger International, 2013).

Looking back, though, our lives would've been totally different if I had gotten that job, and not necessarily in a better way. I would probably still be a police officer. I wouldn't have finished college. We wouldn't have gone to Japan. We wouldn't have met Doug and Thea Wood. I would've been the stereotypical police officer with constant overtime, no time off, and no chance to see my kids at school events.

This was what I'd call an upside-down miracle, one that reinforces your faith not because you get what you want, but because you push through the hurt of not getting what you want and come out the other side to something much better. Our life and God's blessings have been incredible because I didn't get that job.

What's interesting is that I kept testing the side rails to make sure I was in the middle of God's will. Do you think after not getting that job that I let it go?

Of course I didn't.

I applied for other law enforcement jobs, still thinking I'd be a police officer later, tossing a line out there just in case. And the door remained closed, even though I kept applying. Was it a lack of faith that I kept applying?

I don't think so.

I see it more as sowing seed. I often hear Christians say they're going to trust the Lord to bless their business, and then they proceed not to do any work. A farmer with a field won't grow anything if he doesn't toss some seed out into it. Even the little boy brought five loaves and two fish with him to hear Jesus speak and ultimately witness the miracle of that food being used to feed thousands (John 6:1–14). God can take a little and make it a lot, but we still have to show up, ready to plant seed.

God didn't stop there when it came to working in our lives.

In 2012, he made himself very clear to me again. It was when I was considering leaving the police force. Though it wasn't an audible voice, it was as clear as if it had been.

"Kevin, are you going to trust me?" God asked, nudging me to leave my job.

I was pulled toward leading in a new direction. I knew God would take care of us and bless us, but I wasn't sure about whether or not he'd replace my law enforcement income if I quit my job. Not only did God come through, but within months we had recouped that income and then some.

"Do you realize Dylan will never know what it was like to have a dad wake up and go to work?" one of Bekah's friends told her. He was two when I left my law enforcement job, with no memory of the crazy hours. What an incredible blessing, one I couldn't have imagined.

The third time God really worked in my life was in 2017, using John Bevere's book *Relentless: The Power You Need to Never Give Up*. I didn't know who Bevere was at the time, but I'd finished an Audible book and Bevere's book was the only one left to listen to.

Well, I have nothing better to do, I thought and set it to play. And at first, I didn't like it. *This guy's a little off his rocker.*

But I listened and the words worked their way through me. Then, throughout the summer, God led me to podcasts and other teachings that wove well with what I'd read, placing the call to get involved in foster care on me.

Foster care is a lot of work.

Maybe I could just be a mentor to a foster kid, I thought. That would be easier.

But Bevere's words came back to me. When God told Elijah it was going to rain, he sent his servant out seven times to look for the rain (1 Kings 18:42–45). Elijah knew what was going to happen (future), and he led from the future by acting in the now. He took the steps of trusting God.

The first time I went to get Evie, at six weeks old, it was just to help out some friends. I had no intention of anything beyond that temporary help, but when I picked her up, God made it very clear to me.

Me and Evie on her second visit to our house.
I knew she'd be my daughter by now.

The boys loving on Evie during
her first visit in September, 2017.

"Kevin, this is your daughter. Are you going to step up and be her dad?"

It was the same voice I'd heard in 2012.

I knew it was God, but I was overwhelmed because it wasn't what we really wanted to do. The next morning, I asked Bekah about adopting Evie.

"Absolutely not," she said.

"Why don't you pray about it and think it over?" I said, not wanting to press further.

A few weeks later, we decided to go forward with making Evie our daughter. It was then that we discovered that Evie wasn't up for adoption, but was intended to be reunited with her family. Still, we were encouraged to at least be certified as foster parents, and so we began that work. The state allowed us to care for her a few times a week as we worked on the certification before ultimately placing her with us.

Everything was a step of faith. It was completely abnormal for me, but God had said she would be my daughter, so I made sure I acted as such and walked in faith. I led from the future.

The entire situation, from her being reassigned by the state with us as her official foster parents to ultimately being able to adopt, was a series of miracles only possible because of God.

Me and Evie in 2017.

It wasn't easy. There were a lot of seemingly impossible roadblocks, from court cases to delays we hadn't counted on. There were tears, and we questioned God about whether we'd made a mistake.

"This is your daughter," God kept telling us. "You will be her dad."

And I am.

MIRACLES COME WITH ACTS OF OBEDIENCE

When everything is in your control, you don't need a miracle.

The Israelites weren't in control. They couldn't have left Egypt without a miracle, made out of other miracles. They had to follow a cloud or pillar of fire because they didn't know where they were going, and that was its own miracle. God provided them manna to eat, another miracle. The parting of the Red Sea was a huge miracle.

But what gets lost in all of those spectacular miracles were the daily steps they had to take. God didn't pick them all up from Egypt and drop them into the Promised Land. There was a monotony of the day-to-day, being led, obeying, eating the same manna.

God's miracles aren't on our timeline, and they don't happen how we think they should. The miracle of adopting Evie didn't

WHEN EVERYTHING IS IN YOUR CONTROL, YOU DON'T NEED A MIRACLE.

happen instantly and painlessly. It would have been nice if all the red tape had been cut and every door opened at the right time. But we still had to go through the daily struggles and walk the path to get to the end. God was clearly at work every step of the way, but we had to keep taking those steps. We had to keep following the cloud.

The Red Sea wouldn't have parted if the Israelites hadn't made the journey to its shore.

God can do miracles of all kinds, but many times he works within the confines of the physics and systems of the world. When we want instant deliverance from an addiction, he might be leading us through months or years of hard work instead. When we want healing, he might heal, or he might use tremendous difficulty in your life to change you or those around you in some way. Lack of speed or flashy outcome doesn't make it any less of a miracle.

Don't let the unfinished miracles of others get in your way.

Too many people stop taking the steps and sit down instead, insisting that they didn't get their miracle. Miracles aren't a magic wand for an easy life. There are more steps to take after the miracle.

Contending is a big part of uncommon freedom. Some people get their miracle and they take their paddles out of the water and start floating back downstream. A miracle isn't the arrival point; it's part of the journey. It's easy to go back to what you knew. The Israelites were freed, but started thinking they'd like to go back to slavery simply because they had more interesting food to eat.

HONORING THE KING ONE STEP AT A TIME

Honor and worship are connected.

We honor Jesus Christ by how we actually live our lives and make decisions. God prefers our obedience rather than our sacrifice (1 Samuel 15:22).

Knowing that Christ is ultimately in control but that we also have free will is a kind of difficult tension to walk. Uncommon freedom in your faith recognizes this, and balancing on that tension means understanding that obedience requires action and not flowing along with the water headed downstream.

I don't want to say that I have to "do my part" as if God couldn't accomplish his will if my part is missing. Instead, it's a question of obedience and recognizing the opportunities God is giving us.

This brings to mind the story often referred to as the parable of the drowning man. A man stranded on his roof during a flood refuses the rescue attempts of two boats and a helicopter, each time telling the would-be rescuers that he is waiting for God to save him. After turning them all away, he drowns in the flood. When he meets God in Heaven, he asks why God didn't intervene and save him. God responds that he sent the boats and the helicopter to save the man, but that the man didn't see God's work being done right in front of him.

God gives us the opportunity to work with him, where he's working. We can obey and do the work, or we can refuse and miss out on the blessing. If we don't do what God intended for us to do, He will find someone else to do it. And that person will get the blessing God intended for us.

After turning down the last rescue attempt, the man drowns in the flood. After his death, the man meets God and asks why he did not intervene. God responds that he sent all the would-be rescuers to the man's aid on the expectation he would accept the help.

Jesus left us here to do work, and there is much work for us to do. We weren't made to be passive, but we were made to advance. We have an obligation to fight, to be on the offense and charge the gates of hell. We have an obligation to invest what God gives us until we die. Nowhere are we told to retire and sit back and watch the world go by.

The Bible is clear that we are rewarded for our good works, which are going to be judged someday (1 Corinthians 3:10–15).

It's not an attempt to earn my salvation. Doing good works for God is a way we honor him, because who doesn't want to do good things for the person you love?

The funny thing about works is that they become an engine that moves us forward. They build on themselves.

Over the years, I've noticed that when a client pursues better health, their spiritual life often improves as well. Their demeanor changes as they get healthy physically; they open up and become happier people. Doing the work for their health is an engine that affects other parts of their life, and it ends up catching the attention of others around them. People stop and look at things that are marvelous. They notice people going against the current.

Uncommon freedom is so unusual that people can't stop looking at it. They wish for it, but they don't think it's attainable for them in their health, their marriage, their family, or their faith.

I disagree.

The Irish elk is within you.

God created us to be conformed to the image of his Son. God, who is so incredible that Moses had to hide in a rock and only look at the back of his glory or he would die. God, whose voice causes mountains to crumble. God, whose messengers caused people to cower in fear every time they came face-to-face.

We can't settle for being something less.

When the twelve spies were sent into the Promised Land, only two came back and said it could be taken. This was the land God had promised to give the Israelites, but they refused to believe they could stand against the giants in the land. It wasn't humility that caused the ten to say it was impossible. It was a lack of faith. They stopped at "I can't" instead of saying "I can't do it on my own, but I trust God to do it and so I'll take steps forward in faith."

You can take the promised land before you, because God is the one who made the promise. Put your paddle in the water and start rowing.

CHAPTER 9

DESIGN YOUR LIFE

Who do you trust to design your life?

During the pandemic, so much of life was out of our control. We were at the mercy of the government and outside forces at every level, told what we could or couldn't do, where we could or couldn't go. Our family had been in Kenya for the water well dedication when the pandemic really hit the United States. When we got back, it felt as if we were walking onto the set of a zombie movie.

The airports we flew through were ghost towns. When we landed in Phoenix, it seemed deserted. There were hardly any cars on the streets, and the grocery store shelves were practically empty. People were locked down, living life as they were told to, living based on what they were told was safe.

The pandemic did a great job illustrating what life looks like when we let others design it for us.

We don't need a worldwide pandemic to illustrate the point; most of us have plenty of moments where we try to squeeze a life we want into the gaps in the system we're caught in. Early in our marriage, a medical procedure had failed and I was to get a corrective procedure at no expense. But because it was so diffucult to get time off as a police officer, I kept putting it off until we could pair it with a vacation or business trip.

That is not a designed life.

Have you felt like you were living in a perpetual pandemic, where your life was controlled by other people? Where you restricted yourself because of what someone told you was best or safe, making decisions based not on God's calling, but on what others expected of you?

In that kind of life, you don't get to say yes or no. It's a permission-based way of living where others tell you what you're allowed to do. You don't get to control your time. You don't get to go where you want to go and do what you want to do.

Most of us live a life designed by someone else, squeezed into someone else's system, whether we realize it or not. When you *do* realize it, staying in that place is almost unbearable. During the pandemic, we made decisions that were best for our family and that meant deciding to live life very differently than we had before. We weren't going to let others start designing our lives for us.

It's a sad reality, but most people accept the life they're given rather than being brave enough to build the life they want.

THE UNDESIGNED LIFE

Where there is no design, there is chaos.

One of the great aspects of God is that he brings order out of chaos. A life that isn't designed with purpose is a chaotic life.

The average life is controlled by a person's schedule and finances instead of vice versa. Often the answer to opportunities is "no" because your finances or schedule won't allow it—whether you're interested or not.

Vacation time gets squeezed in somewhere, if at all. You feel as if you're surviving (barely) but not thriving. You're in a community you didn't intend to be in, having to work with the default available.

Oddly enough, some people are stuck in an average life because of guilt or pressure. Family, culture, and other traditions define how and where they live. They live a life they're expected to live instead of what they want to live.

The average life is in the grips of what happens to you and around you, instead of what you're creating and making happen. You're a passenger in your own life, definitely not gripping the oars and controlling the course you take.

A life that's completely stuck is all of this, but worse.

Overwhelming anxiety or anger consumes you every day. You're cynical about everything, excited about nothing. You're living for the weekend where you try to cram an entire week of life into two days. You feel like your life is a pointless dead-end that you want out of. You see the health and social history of your family as impossible to break free from.

People trapped in a stuck life spend their free time consuming alcohol and watching a lot of TV. They consume large amounts of social and traditional media, perhaps feeding an addiction to the fear and rage of politics or current events. They hang out with a lot of other stuck people. Stuck people also tend to be consumers and great targets for advertising; they are looking for ways to put happiness and joy in their lives and are chasing products, media, or experiences they think will provide it.

Whether your life is average or stuck, it lacks uncommon freedom and you envy those who have a better life than you. "Must be nice to be so lucky," is how you understand the disparity in your life compared to others. The victim mindset drives your worldview.

Luck has nothing to do with it. But the inability to see the value in designing your own life does. Waiting for handouts or to be given an opportunity instead of creating your own does. These are harsh words, but an undesigned and chaotic life is deadly for you and your family. What grows from that soil finds its way into future generations, and it's not for the best.

In contrast, people living lives of uncommon freedom wake up each day with meaning and purpose.

They've built lives on habits and activities that make this possible. They consistently create new opportunities and invest in the people around them. They are able to do this because they have control of their schedule and their finances, making it possible to say yes or no when they want. They aren't burdened by debt, nor are they controlled by the consumer-driven forces that vie for their attention. While average people pay their own bills and stuck people try to mooch, uncommonly free people are able to pick up the tab if they choose.

The uncommonly free life is one of abundance, not just in money, but in mindset. The future holds promise instead of unbearable monotony.

We are intentional to take at least 3 trips per year as a family.
We love the Bahamas, Cabo, boating and skiing.

You can't get to an uncommonly free life by luck or accident, though.

It happens by design.

WHAT IS LIFESTYLE DESIGN?

The ultimate designer of your life is God.

He designed you specifically for the life He intended for you. The talents he's given you, the doors he's opened for you—it's all part of that design. But when you let outside forces control you, whether through bad decisions or lack of effort, you take the reins away from God and give them to the circumstances around you.

God designed you to go upstream. The world wants you to head in the other direction. Designing your life is simply doing the work that makes it possible for you to be fully available for

LIFE IS
INTENDED
TO HAVE A
PURPOSE, AND
THAT MEANS
WE MUST BE
PURPOSEFUL
ABOUT IT.

what God has for you. Life is intended to have a purpose, and that means we must be purposeful about it. We must be intentional about how we live every day when it comes to our entire being, whether physical, spiritual, or relational.

That's where lifestyle design comes in.

DEFINE YOUR CORE VALUES

Designing comes before building. You don't build a house without a blueprint. If you like lots of light, you'll include windows everywhere you can. If you value privacy, you'll build your house to keep your neighbors from looking in. If you like quiet, your rooms will be smaller. If you have children, you'll include space to play.

We consider how we want to live our lives when we're designing our house.

Yet we often try to build our lives without any sense of design.

In order to build a life of uncommon freedom, you have to design it first, and that requires thoughtful consideration. Remember the saying from John Maxwell that most people accept the life they were given instead of choosing to lead the life they want?

The toughest question is being honest about where you are on the continuum in all of the areas we've covered in this book. Are you stuck? Average?

Then you need to know who you are and what your core values are. What matters the most to you? What are you good at? What gifts and talents has God given you? Who are the five people you spend the most time with? When do you enjoy life the most? What are you doing when you enjoy life the most? What do you want to change? If you weren't limited, if you couldn't fail, what would you do?

You need to move from the thought pattern of "what's the point" to "wow, what if?"

This isn't just from a career standpoint but about your life as a whole. Build a foundation on something you're good at and enjoy most of the time. If you're not sure, ask people who know you best, people you respect.

In my life, identifying my core values was a big turning point. I had an epiphany one day and I realized I valued freedom more than anything. That meant having a job that dictated every aspect of my life clashed with that core value.

Maybe your core values are service to others, which would affect where you live, work, and go to church. Perhaps you want to reach a specific community, and so you want to move there. The point is to figure out what you value the most, determine what's keeping you from it, and then plan accordingly.

In our lives, our finances were keeping us from living according to our number one value of freedom. The first step to living according to our core values meant getting our finances under control.

START HERE:

To help you get started, try this exercise to begin identifying what your core values may be. Do the exercise with your spouse. If your kids are old enough, you might want to include them as a way to identify your family values.

1. Using the words below, underline the top ten values that you identify with. Then, from those ten, circle the top five. Then, put a star next to your top three. If you have it in you, put a square around the top value. Once you have it narrowed down, start thinking about what things in your life you would have to change to begin aligning with your core values.

Abundance	Courage	Loyalty
Freedom	Sustainability	Flexibility
Faith	Self-respect	Assertiveness
Integrity	Health	Minimalism
Generosity	Emotional Stability	Faithfulness
Gratitude	Respectfulness	Fairness
Curiosity	Authenticity	Adventure
Honesty	Kindness	Creativity
Perseverance	Knowledge	Peace
Citizenship	Wisdom	Reputation

2. For even more inspiration, think about what scripture verses you could use in a crest that would correspond with your family values.

TALK TO YOUR PEOPLE

We have some friends who were planning a move from California.

The wife had loved gardening all her life, and her big gardens had made it difficult for their family to travel because the plants required constant watering and upkeep, especially during the hot California summers. For years, the husband helped her with her garden and the wife assumed the husband loved gardening as much as she did. When the time came to move to Alaska to follow their kids and grandkids, the wife asked the husband if he was okay with giving up gardening.

"I've never liked gardening," he told her. "I only did it all these years to support you."

The wife had kept up gardening partly because she thought the husband enjoyed it.

This is the classic "Abilene paradox," where people go along with something assuming the others want to, while the truth

THE SEVEN DISCIPLINES OF UNCOMMON FREEDOM

is that no one does.[23] No one wants to rock the boat, or seem unsupportive, so there is no communication of the truth. For years, instead of taking vacations, a couple stayed home to keep the water sprinklers going for plants that neither of them cared that much about.

An assessment of yourself and your family's situation brings these things into the open. Neither Bekah nor I came from families that put kids in preschool or daycare. It wasn't something we'd considered for our older three boys. But suddenly, with Evie, we found we were parents of a young child again and that our freedom was gone. The business we'd worked so hard to build might disappear, particularly for Bekah, who felt an obligation to be a stay-at-home mom again.

The simple question of "what if" changed everything. What if we put Evie in preschool? Making that move aligned with our core values and relieved tension at home.

START HERE:

How many things in life are you doing for no reason other than you assume it's what's expected of you because you never asked? Ask yourself the following questions:

1. What's one thing you do because you think it's what others expect of you?

2. Is there anything you're doing now because you think you're serving someone, but you haven't communicated with them about the value you both get out of it?

3. If you couldn't fail, what would you change right now? What are your first steps toward achieving this?

---

23. Allaya Cooks-Campbell, "What the Abilene Paradox Is and Ways to Minimize It," BetterUp, October 21, 2022, https://www.betterup.com/blog/abilene-paradox.

GET HEALTHY

Getting healthy plays a big role in being able to design your life.

You might think I keep beating on the same drum, but hear me out.

When you're unhealthy, you're taking on the financial burden of health care costs. When you're unhealthy, you're going to struggle with low energy and brain fog. There's a kind of physical and financial lethargy that comes with being unhealthy, and in that state, you're not going to ramp up any side hustle. You'll barely have the energy to get through the day, much less redesign your life.

Flipping the switch to better health activates change in other parts of your life because health is tied to habits, finances, and how you spend your time.

START HERE:

Do you know what state your health is in currently? Knowing where you are is the key to moving forward. You can start by doing the following:

1. Take the Uncommon Health Assessment[24]

2. Do a current reality check of your health by doing a body fat test either at home[25] or at a facility near you.

3. How can you start "pulling the anchor up" today? Can you take a walk? Eat a healthier dinner?

---

24. www.BekandKev.com/uf-health-assessment.
25. https://inbodyusa.com/.

RE-EVALUATE HOW YOU SPEND YOUR TIME

By looking at your calendar, I can tell you what your priorities truly are. Time is your most valuable asset, your most important resource.

Just as you invest your money you invest your time, and what you put the most time toward is the habit you build. In fact, how you spend your time determines a lot of your health, financial, and relational habits. We talked about the importance of leverage when it came to finances, but the same concept applies to time. Use your time in a way that returns the most value for it.

An average life devalues time.

What if you put a price tag on your time, and then calculated how much time you spend watching Netflix? Are you comfortable spending thousands of dollars each month on Netflix because you're bored?

Spend your time on what you're called to do instead of wasting it or using it on things that deplete your energy.

START HERE:

How can you use your time in a way that returns the most value? Answer the questions below to get started thinking about your time as your most important resource.

1. If you were in control of your schedule, how many hours a day would you:

    a. Sleep

    b. Spend time with your spouse

    c. Spend time with your kids

    d. Exercise

    e. Serve others

f. Work

g. Enjoy hobbies and recreation

THE UNCOMMON FREEDOM TIME BUDGET

MY COMMITTMENTS	SUN	MON	TUE	WED	THU	FRI	SAT	WEEKLY TOTAL
HOURS BUDGETED								/ 168

MANAGE YOUR ENERGY

Imagine a line with "energy giver" on one side and "energy taker" on the other.

There's no shortage of energy takers. Stress. Fighting. Conflict. Distraction. Too many decisions to make. Connections in the wrong circles. People that make an otherwise fun activity something you dread.

For the "energy taker" side, think of delegation, outsourcing, or finding different ways to accomplish what needs to be done. We made the decision to pay for some childcare so that Bekah could work more productively. Before, we'd hired a babysitter now and then for specific events, but now Bekah could be productive when I was at work and not available to help at home. We were intentional to not abdicate our parenting responsibilities to a nanny, but there are plenty of things a nanny can do that allow us to invest in quality time with our kids.

Let's say that summer road construction has made every drive, even just to get groceries, a frustrating time-suck. It's eating up your time *and* energy, making you angry every time you go down the road, so a better option might be to spend a bit more and have groceries delivered.

What worked before (driving to get groceries) doesn't work in the changed environment. You have to constantly manage your energy. During the pandemic, managing our energy was critical to making our way through. To avoid stress points, we had to do things very differently.

On the "energy giver" side of the line, think about what makes your spirit feel more alive. Maybe it's a geographic place you visited and would love to live. Maybe it's a hobby that you love doing more than anything. Maybe there are certain people whose very presence energizes you. Maybe it's as simple as making decisions ahead of time or making changes to reduce the number of decisions you have to make in the day (e.g., Steve Jobs wore the same thing every day) to avoid decision fatigue and keep your energy focused on more important things.

START HERE:

Think about what are "energy takers" and "energy givers" in your own life.

1. Start filling in the list below to identify your energy givers and takers. Add your activities, mark them as a giver or taker, and make sure to identify anyone you should avoid doing that activity with.

2. Once you've made these identifications, can you start to delegate or lessen your energy-draining activities?

THE ⓤ UNCOMMON FREEDOM ENERGY AUDIT

ACTIVITY	ENERGY GIVER? WHY?	ENERGY TAKER? WHY?	ANYONE TO AVOID DOING THIS WITH?

HARNESS AN ABUNDANCE MINDSET

Put on an abundance mindset early in the game.

Thinking precedes creation in your life (Proverbs 23:7). You have to change your mind first to change your life, so get the abundance mindset in place. You might not be at the height of uncommon freedom, but the right mindset is critical to getting there. An abundance mindset works toward a real goal. The rest is just dreaming about a fantasy.

An abundance mindset is in contrast to a scarcity mindset, which sees the world as having limits to what's available. That causes a person to make decisions that are limited, short-term, and even selfish. Limited resources mean hoarding, holding on, and gripping tightly.

Thinking from a position of abundance means we view our future and opportunities as limitless. We can see the long game and understand that stewardship is part of it.

A family we know has a daughter whose dream car is a pink Jeep. For now, though, she has an older model car, one she doesn't like that much. So far, she's had four minor accidents with it, yet still presses her parents for a pink Jeep. Her father asked her why he should help her get her dream car when she's damaged the car she has right now.

"I don't take good care of this car because it's not my dream car," she told him.

The thing is, if you don't take care of the cheap car, you won't take care of your dream car. Being a good steward of what you have now is part of an abundance mindset.

And with an abundance mindset, there's no end to what we can accomplish, and we act accordingly. It's important to remember that in your abundance, what you're given is for a greater purpose than personal enjoyment. It is the *love* of money that is the root of all evil, not the money itself. Loving the power and attention money gives you is not an abundance mindset; it's self-serving and destructive.

A practical application to get you started with an abundance mindset is tithing. If you're not already tithing at least 10 percent, start now. You have to practice being faithful with a little if you expect to do it when you have more, and this is an easy place to start.

An abundance mindset drives you forward. I don't want my standard of living to decrease, but because I've committed to giving more, that standard *will* decrease if I don't grow my business. The abundance mindset creates a structure that forces the drive.

START HERE:

Start thinking from a position of abundance! Answer these questions to get you thinking about moving toward applying the principles of uncommon financial freedom.

1. Are you a good steward of what you have now, even if there's more you want?

2. Is giving a part of your planned finances or is it only if there is "leftover?" Can you use the abundance mindset to change that if needed?

3. Do you ever fight for the check?

4. Think critically about the things you do to "save money" and determine if you are truly saving by putting your time into these things. What could you be spending your time on instead? Could your time be used to actually make money instead of "saving"? Is it something you could easily hire someone else to do or delegate? For example:

    a. Cleaning

    b. Driving to a cheaper grocery store

c. Do-it-yourself home repairs

d. Do-it-yourself car maintenance and repairs

e. Yard work and landscaping

f. Administrative work (emails, filing, etc.)

IT'S OKAY TO DO A REDESIGN

What if your designed life isn't what you like?

Remember, few things are permanent. When you design your life, based on good habits and solid changes, those things transfer. You can do a redesign.

Don't like your new location? Move elsewhere. Don't like your new work? Try something else. The good foundation you've built will carry you through. Don't let a fear of not knowing what you'll like keep you from trying. The old saying "better the devil you know than the devil you don't" means choosing to stick with something less simply because you don't know what the next effort might be like. It also means you're settling for a hellish life.

Consider ways you can test the water before taking the leap, and create a solid decision-making process. When we make big decisions, we talk to people. We value word of mouth from people we respect and admire; we're cautious about whose opinions we get. Bekah and I also make pros and cons lists, and we ask whether or not it will solve a problem or create a problem. Will the decision be one we regret on our deathbeds?

Just remember that a stalled car is easier to steer when it starts moving, even if it's just one or two people pushing the car. You can't have everything figured out ahead of time. You can't wait for all the information before you make a decision. You need to get some movement going.

Designing your life is a balance of your purpose and your preference. Your purpose comes from God. Your preferences are flexible. There's a lot of freedom in that.

HOPING FOR THE FUTURE AT TODAY'S EXPENSE

You could put off designing your life, but why would you?

In 1889, German Chancellor Otto von Bismarck introduced the idea of retirement.[26] He set the retirement age at seventy due to some train wrecks in which the older operators were falling asleep on the job. The catch, though, was that people weren't expected to reach age seventy, and if they did, they probably wouldn't live too long after. Instead of having the older people work until they died, taking up jobs for younger generations, they pushed them into a government-supported subsistence living.

That's where the idea of retirement came from, and that 1889 scenario has had a strange and devastating trickle-down effect on the world and how we think "normal" life should look. We've accepted that model as the right way to view life.

Maybe you've heard the story of the young woman who cut off the ham bone before she put the ham in the oven. When she was asked why she did that, she said her mother had always done so. Come to find out, the only reason the mother had done such a thing was her oven wasn't large enough to fit the ham without cutting the bone.

We easily do what's done before us without asking questions. We follow the pattern—we choose that career, eat that food, celebrate this way, take on that responsibility—all because our

---

26. Kenneth W. Gronbach, "Why Retirement Is a Flawed Concept," Harvard Business Review, April 18, 2016, https://hbr.org/2016/04/why-retirement-is-a-flawed-concept.

family has always done this. For some those family roots are a source of pride, but they can also be a trap. The same can be said of the retirement model.

Author Tim Ferris refers to how we view life as slave, save, retire. You work a job you don't like for fifty years and hope you have the time and money after it to redeem all of those wasted years. You're hoping for a good life later at the expense of the life you have now.

We all know of people who spend their retirement years blowing through their money trying to get their health back. They missed their kids growing up, they were absent at family events, they put in the hours and destroyed their health and tossed as much money into savings and retirement, and when the golden years dawn, they are broken.

The stats for retired law enforcement and military aren't great. Many die just a few years after retirement. They've lived a life of stress, and it accumulated in their physical and mental health. Their identity is tied up in their job and they lose a sense of purpose when they retire.

Lifestyle design is all about intentionally planning to spend more time doing the things you love *right now.* Don't wait until retirement; start designing your life right now, within your means.

Maybe you don't start a business right out of the box, but instead, barter and trade services of things you're good at for things you need to delegate. Get creative. Start taking the initial steps of lifestyle design. Parents: it's especially important for you to start now. You have kids who are watching and learning how to live their future based on what you're doing.

But most of all, don't wait.

I get it. Tomorrow always seems like a better time to start something. Being intentional about how we live life is counterintuitive. Forcing ourselves to microdose on the adversity that comes with designing a life, and then following through, is very much an upstream activity.

Evie jumping off the 12' platform into our pool-just go for it!

Your life now might seem impossible to change, so what's the point of designing something new?

If you can't design your life at level one, you can't design it at five.

Start where you're at, whether you're wealthy or not. The lottery winner with a bunch of money dumped on them won't have a better life. It'll be the same life with a lot more headaches. Blessing and wealth poured into chaos is only greater chaos. A designed life handles blessings well.

Uncommon freedom is a life of both/and. Average life is either/or. A stuck life is neither/nor. What can you start designing today?

THE REST IS UP TO YOU

In ancient Rome, it was common for architects to build their structures with large stone archways (a massive feat, at the time). To ensure these arches remained intact during construction, a temporary wooden support was placed underneath. Once the construction was complete, the wooden support was no longer needed and could be removed, leaving behind a sturdy stone arch.

Interestingly, even centuries later, many builders continued placing these wooden supports beneath their arches despite advancements in construction that made them unnecessary. These builders maintained unnecessary methods even when they no longer held practical relevance.

It's easy to see the waste of time and effort it is to hold onto obsolete methods. But if we zoom out and look at our lives through the same lens, are there any age-old beliefs, traditions, or patterns we continue without ever questioning why? If we're honest, of course there are! And embracing the seven disciplines of Uncommon Freedom starts with asking that question of ourselves.

If you've made it this far, I know the status quo doesn't work for you. You're ready for more because you know you were made for more. It's time to set your standards higher, commit to greater action, and hug the sandpaper of refinement God's going to take you through.

There's no magic bullet. The seven disciplines won't work unless you do. Uncommon Freedom belongs to those who dare to break with the mindsets, habits, and limiting beliefs that no longer serve them. Here's what it's going to take:

DISCIPLINE ONE: GET YOUR BODY ON MISSION

Maximizing your physical health will give you the energy to perform at your best in every facet of life.

DISCIPLINE TWO: MASTER YOURSELF, MASTER YOUR WEALTH

Uncommon Freedom actively loves God by making money *through* stewardship and using money *for* stewardship. In this context, poverty is no virtue and wealth is no vice.

DISCIPLINE THREE: BUILD A BULLETPROOF MARRIAGE

God said it isn't good for people to be alone (Genesis 2:18). Marriage is fundamental to raising godly future generations and is a facet of how we relate to God on this side of heaven.

DISCIPLINE FOUR: PARENT WITH A PURPOSE

C.S. Lewis was spot on when he said, "Children are not a distraction from work, they are simply the most important work." Our purpose as parents isn't simply to make our kids happy or raise them to be well-adjusted. We need to raise them to be godly adults, productive citizens, and better spouses and parents than we are today.

DISCIPLINE FIVE: RUN WITH LIONS

Show me your friends and I'll show you your future. You need people in your life who will push you and support you in the hunt for Uncommon Freedom.

DISCIPLINE SIX: HONOR THE KING

Nothing empties heaven's storeroom of blessing like honoring God first in all things. He blesses what we dedicate to His purposes. We can't out-give, out-serve, or out-love God.

DISCIPLINE SEVEN: DESIGN YOUR LIFE

Have the audacity to build the life you want rather than accepting the life you were given. Lifestyle design is not for the materially wealthy alone, but for all people who want to be the dominant force in their own lives.

THE UNCOMMON FREEDOM MANIFESTO

My friend, embrace those seven disciplines, and you will prosper. But know that the journey isn't for the faint of heart. The prize awaits those guided by the Trinity of Uncommon Freedom: always row upstream, get to one, and upgrade your circle.

I've never heard anyone describe what it takes to find uncommon freedom better than my friend Marty Darracott did in the Uncommon Freedom Manifesto:

Uncommon freedom begins with an uncommon decision.
An uncommon decision requires uncommon discipline.
Uncommon discipline demands uncommon action.
Uncommon action commands uncommon consistency.
Uncommon consistency births uncommon results.
Uncommon results yield uncommon freedom.
And that uncommon freedom should be offered
and duplicated to the next generation.

You have the knowledge. The rest is up to you.

I can't wait to see the life of freedom, impact, and abundance you build.

ACKNOWLEDGMENTS

Several years ago I embraced a transformation leadership principle that states: lead from the future, act in the now. I made the decision to write this book in the second half of 2022 and planned the release date in early 2023, well before I even had a manuscript. My wife knows I get the most done under pressure (although she'd call it being a procrastinator) but I was confident that with a stellar team by my side, it would get done in time!

First, thank you Bekah for being an amazing wife. You spent the first thirteen years of our marriage being 100 percent supportive of my career goals, including being a Marine and then being a cop—two careers that take their toll on the entire family unit. You gave up the comforts of home to follow me halfway around the world, spent well over a year apart from me, spent countless nights alone while I was on duty, and ultimately did the hardest job in the world of being a stay-at-home mom with our three boys in the early years while my job dictated my schedule. You continue to support my many hobbies, dreams, and pursuits and have never put a lid on me. You are also my voice of reason.

As I mentioned earlier, Gary Thomas tells a story about the fact that "the ballet is woman." People go to the ballet to see the women, not a man in tights. A man's job is to help his woman do and be more than she can do and be on her own. Creation was good with Adam, and it was very good after God added Eve to the picture. A man's job is to make the beautiful more beautiful. A man should ask himself: "How do I hold her up and support her? How do I showcase my spouse?" I finally made this shift in 2011 when you launched our health coaching business. That shift was the beginning of the upward trajectory in our lives that led us to achieve the uncommon freedom we want every person to experience.

In ballet, the male lead knows he did his job well when he throws the female lead in the air in the final move and steps back into the shadows while the woman is cheered. Watching you shine in your element as a wife, mother, and dynamic business leader and trainer on stage teaching thousands is as rewarding as any job I've had.

To my amazing kids Carson, Austin, Dylan and Evie: Being a parent is one of the hardest and greatest things in life that has taught me more about God the Father than anything else in life. You guys were part of my initial motivation to get healthy, and so many positive things cascaded down from that decision. I love spending time with each of you and I'm proud of the warriors you are becoming. I pray that we have trained you up in the way that you should go and that your unique "ways" lead to your own life of uncommon freedom.

Mom and Dad, thanks for raising me and imparting the values that are essential to uncommon freedom. Dad, you were the only dad in the neighborhood who played football, midnight tag, and other fun things with us growing up. And a special thank you for capturing the photos of my childhood featured in Chapter 1. You set a great example for me. Mom, you homeschooled me *and* my brothers for years and imparted the strong faith I have needed to navigate life. When you finally had the money, you took us out west to see the Grand Canyon and Lake Powell, and also to Puerto Rico. Those two trips are some of my fondest family memories and inspire me to create similar experiences for our family.

Mom and Dad Eaton, thanks for trusting me with your daughter when we were twenty-one years old and I didn't even have a job. You raised an incredible Proverbs 31 woman that is incredibly rare in today's world. You have always supported us and I'm grateful for the decades of playing cards together while enjoying meaningful conversation.

Teressa McMurray, our family and business thrive because of you. You helped make this book a reality in more ways than I can count. Bek and I can relax when we are working and traveling knowing that our kids are in great hands with you. We are grateful for you and love you like family.

To my brother Mike for being a guy I can bounce ideas off of on a regular basis. We talk about business, leadership, employees, finances, taxes, politics, and faith. As Bek and I grew into uncommon freedom, you and I have had more awesome experiences together than I can count. There are not many people who have the time, freedom, and finances to do some of the amazing things we've done—I wish more people could join us. I'll never forget the epic Sugar Bowl in 2014 when the Buckeyes beat Alabama and then went on to win the first College Football Playoff championship!

To Doug and Thea Wood, thank you for giving us the gift of health and our coaching business. You showed us how to delegate and dream big. You did things I thought were crazy at the time but challenged me to live in abundance. You are two of the most impactful people in my life and I love you both dearly.

To Jared Roth, you took me under your wing when I was navigating the transition from employee to business owner. I learned the difference between capability and capacity from you, and that filter has helped me say "no" to the good so we could say "yes" to the great. You are the most intentional person I know and I owe the implementation of "lifestyle design" to your mentorship.

To my Birdie Bogey BBQ family: Mike, David, Scott, Aunt Kim, Uncle Paul, Ryan, and Keith. Our annual event is something I look forward to every year and I wish every person had an awesome family like we do.

To the Arizona Freedom Crew: Bekah, Doug and Thea, Dan and Megan Valentine, Harold and Sam Prestenbach, Mike and Sumer Morenz, and Shane and Angel Bishop, you all were the crew that kept me sane during the chaos of 2020 and beyond. You are amazing entrepreneurs, parents, spouses, and Christian warriors. Thank you for having my back and being that small minority that isn't afraid to do what's right even when it's not popular.

Thanks to the small group of true leaders that I worked for in my early careers: Bob Gibson, Ben Slothower, Col. Rob Kosid (RIP), Chief Ron Louie (HPD), Rich Goerling (former Lieutenant at Hillsboro Police Department), and Alex Oh (my sergeant at HPD). Leadership is the most scarce resource in our world and you all showed me what it was.

To Joe Hurst, for being one of my best friends and a constant encouragement. You lead the way in marriage, parenting, and business, and are an inspiration to me. When I discuss ideas with you, you push me and help me believe in myself.

To our Raising Awesome Adults small group (Chris and Jihae Watson, Thomas and Becky Goodson, Marc and Kara Gagnon, and Andrew and Cat Whitus), you help us up our parenting game. When we think we're screwing everything up you encourage us and help us realize we aren't too crazy. Chris and Jihae, thanks for leading us to Evie and being the biggest influences on our foster and adoption journey. You two are impact makers!

To our Optavia coaching family, we are where we are because of you. There are few better blessings in life than to work with amazing people you love. There are too many of you to mention, but I'm a better person because of the relationships I have developed with so many of you. We are committed to growing and developing so all of you can experience uncommon freedom if you are willing to do the work.

To the authors who are mentors to me through their books:

To my new friend John Maxwell: *The 5 Levels of Leadership* hit me right between the eyes as a veteran positional leader. The rest of your books are icing on the cake. Getting to know you personally in 2023 has been an absolute privilege and I'm honored to be part of your legacy.

To John Bevere, your book *Relentless* rocked my world. Honestly, I thought you were a little crazy the first time I read it. The second time through empowered my faith. It's so good I listen to it at least once per year. You helped me understand the full meaning of "grace" as God's empowerment for us here on earth. God used the lessons in that book to help me recognize his voice when He said "Kevin, this is your daughter." Meeting you in person in 2022 was a highlight of my life, and I'm grateful for your friendship and authenticity.

To Darren Hardy, *The Compound Effect* was a game changer. Such a simple yet profound book that helped me keep pumping the well just when we were starting to see the water flow. This book is so good I re-read it every January. Your Darren Daily videos are daily fuel for my mind, leadership, and business. We haven't met (yet) but thank you for being my mentor.

To Dave Ramsey, your mantra of "live like no one else so that one day you can live like no one else" is packed full of more wisdom than most people realize. *Financial Peace University* and the *Total Money Makeover* were helpful, but few brands have impacted me as much as your EntreLeadership brand. I believe I've listened to every single EL podcast and consider you my personal business coach. Thank you for being a public figure who isn't afraid to call it like it is. I hope to enjoy a "fellowship stick" with you again in the future.

To Jocko Willink, thank you for *Extreme Ownership* and *The Dichotomy of Leadership*. These books are a great reminder that I am responsible for everything that does and doesn't happen in my life, marriage, family, and business. I also need the daily reminder that discipline equals freedom.

To Daniel Lapin, thank you for *Thou Shall Prosper* and specifically the concept of "prosperity with a purpose." Money makes us more of who we are. Therefore, we need more good people to embrace the call to become prosperous so collectively we can do more good together in this world than the many wealthy forces of evil.

To Henry Cloud, your *Boundaries* books have been a huge blessing in our lives. Learning to say no so we can say yes to better things and learning to prune have helped us focus on the highest leverage activities in our lives.

To the photographers whose photos are featured in this book: Josh and Jennifer Photography (pg. 81 & back cover headshot), Terry Schordock (pg. 75), Spintown Photography (pg. 112), Catelin Photography (pg 74 & 123), and Gracie Charpentier (pg. 145). Your eye for detail in capturing these special moments in our life added so much life to the message and elevated the entire book.

To Jordan Loftis and the entire Story Chorus team who made this book possible, thank you! Getting this into the hands of the public is a dream come true that wouldn't have happened without you. This was the ultimate project in surrounding myself with people who are experts in areas that I am weak in, but collectively we churned out a book that I'm incredibly proud of. I'm already looking forward to the next one . . . after at least a year off.

There are too many others to mention who have positively impacted me and brought me up to a higher level. To all of you, thank you. I've heard it said many different ways: "show me your friends and I'll show you your future self." I'm not done improving, but I'm much improved because of the great people who have influenced and mentored me through the years. Let's stay dedicated to reaching our potential and maximizing our impact to make the world a better place together!

ABOUT THE AUTHOR

Kevin Tinter is a proud husband to his beautiful wife, Bekah, father of three sons and one daughter, co-founder of Bek and Kev LLC, and host of the *Uncommon Freedom* podcast. A veteran of the US Marine Corps and former police officer in Hillsboro, Oregon, Kevin is not only passionate about defending our freedoms but driven to help others achieve freedom in their lives as well.

He and Bekah went from overstressed, overweight, and unhealthy with a net worth of less than $200,000 in 2011 to ultra healthy and wealthy with an eight-figure net worth by 2022. As of 2023, they are giving away nearly 50 percent of their annual gross revenue. Kevin is truly passionate about helping people become better stewards in every aspect of their lives so they can reach their potential, maximize their impact, and find uncommon freedom.

Made in the USA
Las Vegas, NV
10 November 2023

80587562R00115